INVENT YOUR RECIPE

ITALIAN COOKBOOK

80 Italian-American Recipes
Made Your Way

By Thomas J. Papia
Author, Photographer, and Cook

IYR PRESS
North East, MD

Invent Your Recipe: Italian Cookbook

Cover Design By IYR Press
Text copyright © 2024 by Thomas J. Papia
Food Photography copyright © 2024 by Thomas J. Papia
Back Cover Photography copyright © 2024 by The Studio Collection

www.inventyourrecipe.com

All rights reserved. No part of this book may be reproduced or used in any manner without the prior written permission of the copyright owner except for use of quotations in a book review.

Hardcover ISBN 13: 979-8-9901897-2-0
Paperback ISBN 13: 979-8-9901897-0-6
Ebook ISBN 13: 979-8-9901897-1-3

Library of Congress Control Number: 2024934821

IYR Press
North East, MD

To my mom, Vickie. My original culinary teacher. For your love and guidance.

To my nonna, Maria. For your hard work, sacrifice, and culinary traditions.

To my wife, Katherine. For your unwavering support and unconditional love.

start with a base recipe, make a few changes, and invent your recipe.

CREATE | TASTE | INNOVATE

DISCLAIMERS

Thank you for choosing to use the recipes in this cookbook. Please review this section for disclaimers regarding the recipes, food safety, and nutritional information.

Recipe Disclaimers

The recipes in this cookbook have been written, tested, and tasted by me personally. I tried to capture the steps and cooking process to the best of my ability; however, I am not held responsible and make no guarantees for individual outcomes of recipes. There are many factors that could affect the outcome of a recipe, including ingredients, equipment, differences in appliances, cooking temperatures, omissions, and one's own cooking skill. I hope these recipes turn out wonderfully. If they do not, I hope you continue to try and make the recipe with new ingredients and process that work for you.

Food Safety Disclaimers

You are encouraged to use best judgement and you assume full responsibility when cooking with raw ingredients, including, but not limited to, eggs, beef, poultry, and seafood. In addition, if you are not sure about food safety or have any questions or concerns, it is your responsibility to seek food safety information from an official food safety expert or authority.

It is the reader's responsibility to review all ingredients in a recipe before cooking to ensure none of the ingredients may cause potential harm or adverse reaction to anyone preparing or eating the food. This includes, but is not limited to, allergies, pregnancy, dietary restrictions, etc.

Nutrition Disclaimers

I am not a health care professional. Any information presented regarding nutrition is intended to be used for information purposes only. Information regarding nutrition is not medical advice, nor is it intended to serve or replace medical advice. To ensure the most accurate nutritional information, the reader should make calculations based on the specific ingredients they use and seek a medical or nutritional professional for expert guidance and information.

CONTENTS

01   What this Cookbook is <u>NOT</u>

03   About The Cook

05   The Approach

06   Recipe Layout Explained

07   Sauces

14   Starters & Sides

58   Pasta

84   Eggplant

98   Chicken

123   Red Meat

141   Seafood

WHAT THIS COOKBOOK IS NOT

If you are looking for a how-to-do-it-all cookbook, this cookbook is not for you. I will be using common ingredients such as chicken broth and boneless chicken breast in my recipes. If you are looking for the cheapest approach to cooking, this cookbook is not for you. I will not be showing you how to make your own chicken broth, or how to break down a whole chicken into pieces.

If you are looking to learn how to make homemade pasta, ravioli, tortellini, or gnocchi, this cookbook is not for you. I am using simple, readily available ingredients for this cookbook. I believe in creating recipes that are easy to follow with ingredients that are easy to source.

If you are looking for fancy or gourmet recipes, this cookbook is not for you. The recipes in this cookbook use simple ingredients found in most grocery stores. The recipes are user friendly and advanced cooking techniques are not needed. Some of the dishes are great for a dinner party, or to entertain guests, but they are not fancy or gourmet.

If you are looking for recipes written by a famous chef, this cookbook is not for you. I have learned everything I know from doing it. I have had no formal training. I have molded my cooking craft the old-fashioned way. I learn and watch from others, I worked in restaurants, and I learn by trial and error.

If you are looking for sweet and tasty treats, sorry, this cookbook is not for you. I am not a baker or a dessert creator, and I would never pretend to be one. I intend to work on the craft of desserts and baking. Until that craft is good enough for paper, I will not be offering dessert recipes.

If you are looking for a new approach to eating, this cookbook is not for you. I will not be offering the latest eating trend or detailed nutritional information. I will offer simple meals with great taste and comfort.

If you are looking for a culinary history of Italy and how each dish represents a different location or sub-culture, this cookbook is not for you. I am first generation Italian American. My recipes are adaptations of the food I have been eating most of my life.

If you are looking for an encyclopedia of 600 Classic Italian Recipes, sorry, this cookbook is not for you. I have focused on the recipes that represent myself and my cooking style.

If you are looking for rigid recipes that give you one, and only one, way to make a dish, this cookbook is not for you. I am not offering one recipe, cooked ten different ways. What I am offering are the recipes that I enjoy cooking and the ingredients that I have changed to make different recipe variations. Choose one suggestion or choose them all. Better yet, choose an ingredient of your own. It is up to you to invent the recipe that works best for you.

If you are looking for exact preparation and cooking times for each recipe, this cookbook is not for you. Everyone prepares and cooks food at different rates. A seasoned chef and the avid home cook will chop vegetables differently. One person's oven may be different in heating efficiency than another's. This may produce different cooking times and outcomes. This cookbook will offer a range of preparation and cooking times to help provide the framework for your meal. I can tell you firsthand that my preparation times has increased with the birth of each of my children. Chopping vegetables is a bit more challenging and time consuming when you are keeping a watchful eye on your children.

If you are looking for precise ingredient measurements, this cookbook is not for you. Precise measurements go against the foundational principle of my method, "Create, Taste, Innovate." I will provide a common measure of ingredients, such as medium onion, or a range of a measurement, such as 12-16 ounces of marinara sauce. These recipes and cooking methods are not bound by precise measurements. Feel free to follow the recipe as written, or, for example, use two medium onions instead of one if you like onions. Invent Your Recipe!

If you are looking for simple recipes and variations, which are full of flavor and comfort, this cookbook <u>IS</u> for you!

ABOUT THE COOK

I am first generation Italian American. My dad and his family came to this wonderful country in 1963 from Favara, Sicily. With them, they brought their culture and cuisine. Through the years, their food and culture united with American food and culture. By the time I was born in 1985, the food that they ate was a little bit Sicilian, Italian, and American.

I have been cooking for about thirty years, dating back to the first time I helped my mom make Sunday dinner. I was about six years old. I remember helping my mom crush whole plum tomatoes with my little hands. Then she would use them in the marinara sauce.

From there, my interest in food and cooking developed. I would cook with my mom every chance that I got. I learned a lot from her, especially how to make quick, flavorful dishes using everyday ingredients without recipes. I also learned a lot from my grandma (Nonna). I have fond memories as a kid watching her cook, and then as I grew up, helping her in the kitchen. She spoke very little English and yet we understood each other completely and our relationship grew from cooking. In the years since she passed away, I have tried my best to honor her memory. I continue cooking her dishes and creating dishes inspired by her. I plan to continue the tradition and pass them on to my children and other family members.

As I got older and started to cook on my own, I found that I did not like following recipes. They were too rigid; I did not like reading all the instructions. I did not understand most of the fancy cooking terms. I took the food and made it the way I could. If I made a mistake and the dish turned out terrible, I learned from it and moved on.

I am a semi-trained cook and not a professional chef. I am an avid food lover who has spent many years making great tasting food for family and friends. My nine-to-five job is in information technology, but my main hobby and passion is cooking. The joy that I get from preparing a meal for another person and seeing their satisfaction is very fulfilling. I love to share that joy and fulfillment with others.

I do have a history of working with food. My first job was working at an Italian deli and caterer. I was fifteen years old and worked one day a week: Sundays. This is where I began to pair my love of food and cooking with some sort of semi-formal instruction. This instruction was in the form of "watch what I do." The owner and staff at the deli were not formally trained. They had businesses for years and passed down their techniques through generations. The only semi-trained employees were the butcher and head cook.

At the deli, they started me with basic tasks, and I had to work my way up to more responsibility. The first year of my training, I washed dishes, cleaned equipment, and mopped floors. I also chopped parsley, basil, garlic, and onions, and grated cheese and stale Italian bread to make breadcrumbs. I would watch and learn from the cook and butcher every chance that I could. I would volunteer to do the messy jobs, like cleaning the meat grinder and grease trap, all so I could spend some time learning from them.

A picture of myself at 16 years old working and learning at the deli. I didn't realize it at the time, but working there formed a solid cooking foundation out of my raw desire and love to make food.

After that first year, I earned more responsibility. My cooking ability and confidence improved. Over the next four years, I earned even more responsibility. This led to me working without supervision. Before I knew it, I was able to cook Italian dishes for parties, prepare cuts of meat for sale, and make many varieties of deli salads and sandwiches. Also, I was learning and running many aspects of the business.

In college, I needed an outlet to continue my journey and my love for cooking. I decided to cater parties part time. When I had the time, I would cook the food, have a lot of fun, and make some money. When I moved on to my graduate education, I decided to work at a local restaurant. I wanted to learn the "whole" picture of cooking as a profession and as a business. Up to that point in my life, I was on the fence about whether to have a career in information technology or food. After two years in the kitchen and obtaining my master's degree, I decided to focus on my career in IT. I did maintain cooking as a hobby and passion.

After a few years and promotions, I found myself wanting more from cooking. Yet, now with a family to support, I needed to maintain my main source of income. That is when I decided to create a food blog and share my ideas. The blog, inventyourrecipe.com, is a passion project of mine and has been very enjoyable for the past five years. Now, I want to achieve a longtime goal of mine and publish a cookbook.

THE APPROACH

The concept of **"Invent Your Recipe"** is all about starting with a base recipe, making a few changes, and inventing the recipe that works best for you.

The driving force for this concept is my family and friends. Countless times I have been asked for my recipes and many of my friends were surprised when I told them I didn't use any. That is when the idea for the "Invent Your Recipe" method of Create, Taste, Innovate and a food blog came to fruition. The concept for my recipe structure began when I was trying to write down steps and ingredients for my wife. She wanted to cook the dishes I love and to be able to change the ingredients based on what was available in the house. The name "Invent Your Recipe" was a direct result of the idea of creating a recipe that works best for you.

My love of food originates with my Italian family and cooking with my mom and grandma (Nonna). "Invent Your Recipe" is the larger concept that I have based my food blog on. For this cookbook, I am focusing on my Italian recipes. These recipes are the ones that I made as a young cook, the first recipes that I have written down, and they are dear to my heart.

This cookbook will provide my favorite Italian recipes written with simple, straight-forward steps. The cookbook will also offer simple suggestions and ingredient alternatives. These alternatives will provide ideas for how the cook can invent the recipe that they enjoy the most. There is no special equipment needed or unique ingredients to buy. These recipes are family and home cook friendly.

Cooking can be a lot of fun; add a little of this, change a bit of that, and before you know it, you have great tasting food. That is what I want this concept and cookbook to portray: the idea that when you invent your recipe, the recipes simply become guidelines. The recipes offer the framework for how you can create simple, great tasting food that you enjoy preparing and sharing.

RECIPE LAYOUT EXPLAINED

Title

SERVING SIZE: This will de displayed as either "Serves" or "Yields"

INGREDIENTS:

This section will have all of the ingredients listed for the recipe. In this section, there will also be ingredient substitute options highlighted in different colors. Each highlighted ingredient will then have an arrow pointed to the ingredient's substitute option, which will also be highlighted in the same color. See below for an example.

2 cups of heavy cream → or light cream
1/2 cup grated parmesan cheese → or asiago cheese
1/2 cup grated Romano cheese
4 cloves of garlic minced
1/2 stick of butter

INSTRUCTIONS:

This section will have all of the instructions for the recipe. The recipe process will be further broken down into smaller instruction sections, such as, "Preparing the Sauce" or "Cooking the Chicken" or "Breading the Eggplant" or "To Serve" or "Approximate Prep Time"

SAUCES

INTRODUCTION TO SAUCES

I love making sauce! Sauce is the foundation of so many great dishes, and I use five main sauces in mine: Alfredo, Bolognese, Marinara, Roasted Tomato, and Vodka. A simple, well-seasoned, well-balanced sauce is a staple in many of my Italian recipes. A fantastic sauce can stand alone on its own as a star. It can also transform and elevate some of the more traditional and basic recipes.

Alfredo sauce is not my personal favorite. Yet, this Alfredo recipe will delight and pair well with fettuccini and chicken. The Bolognese recipe is great for a quick sauce. I enjoy making Bolognese to pair with linguine or rigatoni for a hot lunch or weeknight dinner. I often use ground turkey or chicken instead of ground beef in the Bolognese. It is a nice way to change the recipe and incorporate a leaner meat.

What can I say about my vodka sauce recipe? Yum! The flavors, the creaminess, the way the sauce sticks to the pasta, it is all so wonderful and delicious. Penne a la Vodka is a family tradition on Christmas Eve. We make the traditional fish and have chicken cutlets and Penne a la Vodka for the non-fish eaters. As a child, I couldn't wait until Christmas Eve to have my cousin's vodka sauce! When I started cooking, this was one of the things I wanted to learn to make, and I wanted it to be as delicious as possible. Over the years, I've tried changing up the ratio of the ingredients. I have used different tomatoes and cream (light, whole, half-and-half). The recipe I am sharing in this cookbook is the result: it is tried, tested, and family and friends approved. I hope you enjoy it.

Have fun making these great tasting sauces. Each sauce can be used as an ingredient to create so many wonderful dishes. If you can perfect all, or even one of these sauces, you will add another layer of depth to your skills as a cook.

ALFREDO SAUCE

SERVES 4

INGREDIENTS:

1/2 stick unsalted butter
4 garlic cloves, minced
2 cups of heavy cream *(or light cream)*
1/2 cup grated parmesan cheese *(or asiago cheese or sharp provalone)*
1/2 cup grated Romano cheese
1/4 cup chopped fresh parsley
1/4 teaspoon ground black pepper

INSTRUCTIONS:

PREPARING THE SAUCE:

In a large skillet, melt the unsalted butter on medium heat. Next, add the minced garlic and sauté until golden in color, about 1-2 minutes, being careful not to burn the garlic. Continuing on medium heat, add the heavy cream, bring to a simmer, and cook for 5 minutes, stirring occasionally. Next, add the parmesan cheese, Romano cheese, fresh parsley, and black pepper. Bring to a simmer and cook for 8-10 minutes, stirring occasionally, until the sauce thickens.

TO SERVE:

Mix with your favorite pasta and enjoy.

APPROXIMATE PREP TIME:	5-10 minutes
APPROXIMATE COOK TIME:	20-30 minutes

BOLOGNESE SAUCE

SERVES 4

INGREDIENTS:

1 pound ground beef (80/20) — *or ground turkey, chicken, or pork*

1 stick unsalted butter

4 garlic cloves, sliced

1 can (28 ounces) crushed tomatoes

1/4 cup grated Romano cheese — *or grated Parmigiano Reggiano*

1 teaspoon dried oregano

1/2 teaspoon salt

1/4 teaspoon ground black pepper

INSTRUCTIONS:

PREPARING THE GROUND BEEF:

In a large skillet on high heat add the ground beef. Cook until ground beef is browned and no longer pink, about 5-7 minutes. Ensure you are breaking apart the meat and mixing occasionally. When the ground beef is done, remove from the heat.

PREPARING THE SAUCE:

While the ground beef is cooking, melt the unsalted butter in a medium sauce pot. Next, add in the garlic and sauté until golden, about 1-2 minutes. Next, add in the crushed tomatoes, grated cheese, oregano, salt, and ground black pepper. Bring to a simmer and cook for 20 minutes. Next, add in the cooked ground beef and simmer for 10 minutes, stirring occasionally.

TO SERVE:

Mix with your favorite pasta and enjoy.

APPROXIMATE PREP TIME: 5-10 minutes

APPROXIMATE COOK TIME: 35-40 minutes

MARINARA SAUCE

YIELDS ABOUT 5 QUART-SIZE MASON JARS

INGREDIENTS:

- 1/4 cup extra virgin olive oil
- 10 garlic cloves, sliced
- 2 medium sweet onions, diced
- 1/2 cup red wine
- 1/2 cup water
- 1 can (6 ounces) tomato paste
- 2 teaspoons dried oregano
- 2 teaspoons salt
- 1 teaspoon dried basil
- 1 teaspoon ground black pepper
- 4 cans (28 ounces) crushed tomatoes *(or whole plum tomatoes (crushed) or tomato puree)*
- 1/2 cup of grated Romano cheese
- 2 tablespoons sugar *(or 2 medium carrots, minced)*

INSTRUCTIONS:

PREPARING THE SAUCE:

Place a large pot over medium heat and add the extra virgin olive oil. Next, add in the garlic and sauté until golden, about 2-3 minutes. Next, add the onions and sauté for 5 minutes until the onions begin to soften, mixing occasionally. Next, add the red wine, water, tomato paste, dried oregano, dried basil, salt, and ground black pepper. Incorporate all ingredients by stirring occasionally and cook for 5 minutes. Next, add the crushed tomatoes and sugar. Bring to a simmer, then reduce to low heat. Simmer for 1 hour, stirring as needed to prevent the sauce from sticking to the bottom of the pot. Next, add the grated Romano cheese and simmer for an additional 1 hour, stirring as needed to avoid the sauce from sticking to the bottom of the pot.

TO SERVE:

Place sauce over a bed of your favorite cooked pasta (I recommend spaghetti).

APPROXIMATE PREP TIME: 20-30 minutes

APPROXIMATE COOK TIME: 2 1/2 hours

ROASTED TOMATO PIZZA SAUCE

YIELDS ENOUGH FOR TWO 14" PIZZAS

INGREDIENTS:

1 can (28 ounces) crushed tomatoes *(or tomato puree)*

1/4 cup extra virgin olive oil

4 garlic cloves, whole

1 teaspoon salt

1/2 teaspoon dried oregano

1/2 teaspoon dried basil

1/2 teaspoon ground black pepper

9 x 9-inch baking dish

INSTRUCTIONS:

Pre-heat the oven to 425 degrees.

PREPARING THE SAUCE:

In a 9 x 9-inch baking dish combine all the ingredients and mix well. Cover the baking dish with aluminum foil and roast for 30 minutes. Stir the sauce and roast for an additional 30 minutes, covered. Finally, remove the foil and roast the sauce for another 10 minutes, or until the top begins to brown. Remove the baking dish from the oven and allow the sauce to cool completely before using with pizza dough.

TO SERVE:

Spread the desired amount of sauce evenly over rolled out pizza dough. This recipe should yield enough sauce for two 14-inch pizzas. Alternatively, this sauce serves well when paired with an appetizer for dipping.

APPROXIMATE PREP TIME: 5-10 minutes

APPROXIMATE COOK TIME: 60-70 minutes

VODKA SAUCE

YIELDS ABOUT 6 QUART-SIZE MASON JARS

INGREDIENTS:

1 stick unsalted butter
10 garlic cloves, sliced
1/2 pound of pancetta, diced *(or prosciutto)*
2 medium sweet onions, diced
1 can (6 ounces) tomato paste
1 teaspoon dried oregano
1 teaspoon dried basil
2 teaspoons salt
1 teaspoon ground black pepper
4 cans (28 ounces) crushed tomatoes *(or tomato puree)*
1 cup water
2 tablespoons sugar
1/2 cup of vodka (80 proof)
1 cup of grated Romano cheese
1-quart heavy cream *(or light cream)*

INSTRUCTIONS:

PREPARING THE SAUCE:

Place a large pot on medium heat and melt the unsalted butter. As the unsalted butter melts, add the garlic and pancetta. Sauté for 5 minutes on medium heat, until garlic and pancetta begin to brown, mixing occasionally. Next, add the onions and sauté for 5 minutes until the onions begin to soften, mixing occasionally. Next, add the tomato paste, dried oregano, dried basil, salt, ground black pepper, and water. Incorporate all ingredients by stirring occasionally and cook for 5 minutes. Next, add in the crushed tomatoes and sugar. Bring to a simmer and reduce to low heat. Simmer for 1 hour, stirring as needed to avoid the sauce from sticking to the bottom of the pot. Next, add the heavy cream, vodka, and grated Romano cheese. Bring to a simmer again and cook for an additional 1 hour, stirring as needed to avoid the sauce from sticking to the bottom of the pot.

TO SERVE:

Place sauce over a bed of your favorite cooked pasta (I recommend penne).

APPROXIMATE PREP TIME: 20-30 minutes
APPROXIMATE COOK TIME: 2 1/2 hours

STARTERS & SIDES

INTRODUCTION TO STARTERS & SIDES

Who doesn't like a good appetizer or side dish? I know I do, and sometimes I make a few of these recipes for my main meal. While I was working in the Italian deli, I learned how to prepare these starters and side dishes. I personalized them a bit throughout the years. For the most part, the essence of the recipes has remained the same.

These starters and side dish recipes are great to pair with an entrée or to bring to a dinner party. They are usually prepared in less than thirty minutes, but some take longer. For instance, arancini (rice balls) with cheese, potato croquettes, and stuffed artichokes are not difficult to make, but they are time consuming. They may take longer to prepare but are favorites of my family and friends.

A favorite dish in this section is broccoli rabe (rapini). The taste may not be for everyone, but the vegetable's unique flavor is wonderful.

Another favorite dish in this section is the rotini pasta salad. In fact, this is the most requested side dish for me to bring to a family or friend's party. The combination of colors and flavors is outstanding. Sometimes I will even make this dish as my main meal. The ingredient possibilities in this recipe really are endless. I have offered a few of my favorite combinations. I encourage you to have fun and pick the ingredients you like the most for this rotini pasta salad.

A unique dish in this section is cacuzza stew. This Italian squash (actually, it is a gourd) is not commonly found in grocery stores or food markets. It is grown in home gardens. I grow my cacuzza and have been taught this recipe by my mom, who learned it from my Nonna. This recipe is special for me to share.

Have fun cooking these starters and sides. There are a wide variety of recipes in this section to choose from. Pick a few of your favorites, give them a try, and then invent the starter or side dish recipe that works the best for you.

ARANCINI - RICE BALLS WITH CHEESE

YIELDS ABOUT 3 DOZEN

INGREDIENTS:

3 cups white rice *(or brown rice)*

6 cups chicken broth *(or vegetable broth or water)*

2 pounds ricotta cheese

2 cups shredded mozzarella cheese *(or asiago cheese)*

1/2 cup grated Romano cheese

1 teaspoon salt

1/2 teaspoon ground black pepper

1 teaspoon garlic powder

4-6 eggs

1/2 cup water

2-3 cups plain breadcrumbs

2-3 cups canola oil

INSTRUCTIONS:

PREPARING THE RICE:

In a rice cooker or large pot, cook the rice according to the package instructions (substitute chicken broth for water). After rice is done, place in a large mixing bowl and let cool in the refrigerator for 1 hour.

PREPARING THE RICE MIXER:

Remove the bowl of rice from the refrigerator and add the ricotta cheese, mozzarella cheese, Romano cheese, salt, ground black pepper, and garlic powder. Mix all the ingredients well. Next, with your hands, form meatball-size rice balls and place on a baking sheet. Allow formed rice balls to cool in the refrigerator until firm enough to bread and fry, about 2 hours. For best results, allow formed rice balls to sit in the refrigerator overnight.

ARANCINI - RICE BALLS WITH CHEESE...CONTINUED

BREADING THE RICE BALLS:

Once rice balls have reached desired firmness prepare an egg wash by whisking the eggs and water together in a mixing bowl. In another mixing bowl, place 2 cups of breadcrumbs (use more as needed). Next, dredge a rice ball into the egg wash and then breadcrumbs, then back into the egg wash, and then breadcrumbs a second time to create a double-coat. Repeat this process until all the rice balls have a double-coating of breadcrumbs.

COOKING THE RICE BALLS:

In a large skillet add 2 cups of canola oil (use more as needed) and bring to a high heat. When the oil is ready, add a layer of rice balls to the frying pan, ensuring the skillet is not over-crowded. Fry the rice balls until golden brown on all sides, about 2-3 minutes per side. Remove the finished rice balls to a tray to cool. Repeat this process until all rice balls have been cooked.

TO SERVE:

Place rice balls on a serving platter with marinara sauce as a dipping option and serve as an appetizer or side dish.

APPROXIMATE PREP TIME:	4-5 hours
APPROXIMATE COOK TIME:	60-70 minutes

Arancini Siciliano

ARANCINI SICILIANO - RICE BALLS WITH MEAT

YIELDS ABOUT 2 DOZEN

INGREDIENTS:

- 3 cups white rice *(or brown rice)*
- 6 cups chicken broth *(or vegetable broth or water)*
- 3 cups (24 ounces) marinara sauce
- 1 pound ground beef *(or ground turkey, chicken, or pork)*
- 2 cups frozen sweet peas
- 2 cups shredded mozzarella cheese *(or asiago cheese)*
- 1/2 cup grated Romano cheese
- 1 teaspoon salt
- 1/2 teaspoon ground black pepper
- 4-6 eggs
- 1/2 cup water
- 2-3 cups plain breadcrumbs
- 2-3 cups canola oil

INSTRUCTIONS:

PREPARING THE RICE:

In a rice cooker or pot, cook the rice according to the package instructions (substitute chicken broth for water). After rice is done, place in a large mixing bowl and add 2 cups of marinara sauce and mix well. Let cool in the refrigerator for 1 hour.

PREPARING THE FILLING:

Bring a medium skillet to high heat. Next, add in the ground beef and cook for 5 minutes, ensuring to break up the ground beef well. Next, add the frozen sweet peas and cook for 4 minutes, stirring occasionally. Finally, add 1 cup of marinara sauce and cook for 2 minutes, stirring occasionally. Remove the skillet from the heat and set aside to cool.

ARANCINI SICILIANO - RICE BALLS WITH MEAT...CONTINUED

FORMING THE RICE BALLS:

Remove the bowl of rice from the refrigerator and add the mozzarella cheese, Romano cheese, salt and ground black pepper. Mix all ingredients well. To make each rice ball, first, use your hands to form a meatball-size ball, then push into the center with your thumb to form a divot. Second, spoon in enough ground beef mixture to fill the divot (about 1 tablespoon) Third, place additional rice mixture (about 1 tablespoon) over divot and roll in hands to form a larger ball and encase the beef mixture. Repeat this process until all the rice balls are formed. Next, allow formed rice balls to cool in the refrigerator until firm enough to bread and fry, at least 2 hours. For best results, allow formed rice balls to sit in the refrigerator overnight.

BREADING THE RICE BALLS:

Once rice balls have reached desired firmness, prepare an egg wash by whisking the eggs and water together in a mixing bowl. In another mixing bowl, place 2 cups of breadcrumbs (use more as needed). Next, dredge a rice ball into the egg wash and then breadcrumbs, then back into the egg wash, and then breadcrumbs a second time to create a double-coat. Repeat this process until all the rice balls have a double-coating of breadcrumbs.

FRYING THE RICE BALLS:

In a large skillet, add 2 cups of canola oil (use more as needed) and bring to a high heat. When the oil is ready, add a layer of rice balls to the frying pan, ensuring the skillet is not over-crowded. Fry the rice balls until golden brown on all sides, about 3 minutes a side. Move the finished rice balls to a tray to cool. Repeat this process until all rice balls have been cooked.

TO SERVE:

Place rice balls on a serving platter with marinara sauce as a dipping option and serve as an appetizer or side dish.

APPROXIMATE PREP TIME: 4-5 hours
APPROXIMATE COOK TIME: 60-70 minutes

BROCCOLI RABE

SERVES 4

INGREDIENTS:

4 broccoli rabe bushels
1/2 cup extra virgin olive oil *(or canola oil)*
6 garlic cloves, sliced
1-2 cups chicken broth *(or vegetable broth)*
1/2 teaspoon salt
1/2 teaspoon ground black pepper
1/2 teaspoon crushed red pepper flakes

INSTRUCTIONS:

PREPARING THE BROCCOLI RABE:

Begin by removing the bottom third portion of each broccoli rabe stem and washing the rabe thoroughly.

COOKING THE BROCCOLI RABE:

In a large pot on high heat, add in the extra virgin olive oil. Next, add the garlic and sauté until golden, about 1-2 minutes. Lower to medium heat and add one half of the broccoli rabe, 1/2 cup of chicken broth, salt, and ground black pepper. Sauté until the broccoli rabe is reduced by half; then add the remaining broccoli rabe, 1/2 cup of chicken broth, and crushed red pepper flakes. Bring to a simmer and cover. Continue to simmer until the broccoli rabe is reduced by half, mixing occasionally. Add additional chicken broth if needed. Serve once stems are tender to the touch or your desired doneness.

TO SERVE:

Serve this dish as an appetizer with some crunchy Italian bread, or as a side dish with your favorite meat or seafood recipe.

APPROXIMATE PREP TIME: 10-15 minutes

APPROXIMATE COOK TIME: 20-30 minutes

BRUSCHETTA

SERVES 4

INGREDIENTS:

6 plum tomatoes, diced — *or roasted red peppers or artichoke hearts*

1/2 small red onion, diced — *or sweet onion*

3 garlic cloves, sliced

1/2 cup extra virgin olive oil

1/4 cup of red wine vinegar

1/4 cup thinly sliced fresh basil

2 tablespoons balsamic vinegar

1/2 teaspoon salt

1/4 teaspoon ground black pepper

INSTRUCTIONS:

PREPARING THE BRUSCHETTA:

In a large mixing bowl, combine all ingredients and mix thoroughly to incorporate.

TO SERVE:

Toast thin slices of Italian bread and spoon the desired portion of bruschetta onto each slice. Alternatively, use the bruschetta as an addition to a salad or as an ingredient in a main entrée.

APPROXIMATE PREP TIME: 15-25 minutes

CACUZZA STEW

SERVES 4

INGREDIENTS:

1 large cacuzza *(or 4 medium zucchini)*

1 can (28-35 ounces) whole peeled tomatoes *(or 2 cans (15-16 ounces) diced tomatoes)*

1/4 cup extra virgin olive oil

4 garlic cloves, sliced

1 medium sweet onion, diced

2 teaspoons salt, divided

1/2 teaspoon ground black pepper

6 large eggs

2 tablespoons sliced fresh basil

Grated Romano cheese to serve

INSTRUCTIONS:

PREPARING THE CACUZZA:

Begin by peeling the skin of the cacuzza and cutting it into bite-size pieces. In a separate bowl, crush the whole tomatoes with your hands and set aside. In a large pot, add the extra virgin olive oil and bring to a high heat. Add the garlic and onions and sauté for 3 minutes, mixing occasionally. Next, add the cacuzza, 1 teaspoon of salt, and ground black pepper and sauté for 5 minutes, mixing occasionally.

BRINGING EVERYTHING TOGETHER:

Continuing on high heat, add the tomatoes and bring to a simmer. Cook for 20 minutes, mixing occasionally. Next, add the eggs and let cook for 1 minute without mixing. Then, mix the eggs into the stew. Bring the stew back to a simmer and cook for 15 minutes, mixing occasionally. At this point taste the stew, and if needed, mix in the additional 1 teaspoon of salt. Finally, turn off the heat, add in the basil, and mix well.

TO SERVE:

Serve as a main entrée with crunchy Italian bread or over pasta for an alternative option. Add grated Romano cheese to taste.

APPROXIMATE PREP TIME: 10-15 minutes

APPROXIMATE COOK TIME: 40-45 minutes

Escarole and Beans

ESCAROLE AND BEANS

SERVES 4

INGREDIENTS:

2 bunches escarole

1/2 cup extra virgin olive oil

6 garlic cloves, sliced

2 cups chicken broth *(or vegetable broth)*

1/2 teaspoon salt

1/2 teaspoon ground black pepper

2 cans (15-16 ounces) cannellini beans (with liquid) *(or great northern or navy beans)*

INSTRUCTIONS:

PREPARING THE ESCAROLE:

Begin by removing the bottom 1-2 inches of each escarole bunch and cleaning thoroughly with water.

COOKING THE ESCAROLE:

In a large pot on high heat, add the extra virgin olive oil. Next, add the garlic and sauté until golden, about 1-2 minutes. Lower to medium heat and add half of the escarole, 1 cup of chicken broth, salt, and ground black pepper. Sauté until the escarole reduces by half, about 3-5 minutes, while mixing occasionally. Next, add remaining escarole and 1 cup of chicken broth. Bring to a simmer and cover. Simmer until the escarole is reduced by half, about 3-5 minutes, while mixing occasionally. Finally, add the cannellini beans, bring to a simmer, and cook for 5 minutes, mixing occasionally.

TO SERVE:

Serve as a main entrée with crunchy Italian bread, or as a side dish with your favorite meat or seafood recipe.

APPROXIMATE PREP TIME: 10-15 minutes

APPROXIMATE COOK TIME: 20-25 minutes

FRIED CAULIFLOWER

SERVES 4

INGREDIENTS:

1 large head of cauliflower *(or 4 cups broccoli florets or 24 ounces green beans)*

2 cups of seasoned breadcrumbs

1/2 teaspoon salt

1/4 teaspoon ground black pepper

1/2 teaspoon garlic powder

1/2 teaspoon onion powder

2-3 eggs

1/2 cup water

1/4 cup grated Romano cheese *(or Parmigiano Reggiano)*

2 cups canola oil

INSTRUCTIONS:

PREPARING THE CAULIFLOWER:

Clean the cauliflower with cold water then cut into 2 x 2-inch pieces. Next, in a mixing bowl, combine the breadcrumbs, salt, ground black pepper, garlic powder, and onion powder and mix well. In another mixing bowl add the eggs, water, and grated Romano cheese and whisk together forming an egg wash. For each piece of cauliflower, dredge in the egg wash, then breadcrumbs, back into the egg wash a second time, and then back into the breadcrumbs to form a double-coat. Repeat until all the cauliflower pieces are coated in this manner. Place breaded cauliflower onto a large tray or dish to stage for frying.

FRIED CAULIFLOWER...CONTINUED

FRYING THE CAULIFLOWER:

In a large skillet, add the canola oil and bring to a high heat. Place the cauliflower into the skillet leaving enough room not to crowd the pan (about 1/2-inch space between pieces). Lower to medium heat and cook for 4 minutes or until golden brown. Next, flip the cauliflower over and cook for another 4 minutes or until golden brown. Remove each piece from the pan and strain on paper towel. Repeat this process until all the cauliflower pieces are cooked.

TO SERVE:

Serve as an appetizer with your favorite dipping sauce, or as a side dish with your favorite meat or seafood. In my family, this fried cauliflower is served with Thanksgiving dinner as a side dish.

APPROXIMATE PREP TIME:	10-20 minutes
APPROXIMATE COOK TIME:	15-25 minutes

Fried Ravioli

FRIED RAVIOLI

SERVES 4

INGREDIENTS:

- 1 cup plain breadcrumbs
- 1-2 eggs
- 1/4 cup water
- 1 package of frozen ravioli *(or frozen tortellini)*
- 1/2 cup canola oil
- 8-16 ounces marinara sauce *(or vodka sauce or alfredo sauce)*
- Grated Romano cheese to taste

INSTRUCTIONS:

BREADING THE RAVIOLI:

In a mixing bowl add the breadcrumbs. In another mixing bowl add the eggs and water and whisk to form an egg wash. For each frozen ravioli, dredge in the egg wash and then the breadcrumbs. Repeat until all the ravioli are breaded. Place breaded ravioli onto a large tray or dish to stage for frying. If frying later, place the breaded ravioli in the freezer to keep frozen.

COOKING THE RAVIOLI:

Place a large skillet on high heat and add in the canola oil. When the oil is hot, add the breaded frozen ravioli to the skillet and fry on both sides until golden brown in color, 2-3 minutes each side, ensuring not to crowd the skillet. Remove ravioli from the skillet and set aside. Repeat this process until all the ravioli is cooked.

TO SERVE:

Serve as an appetizer or a side dish. Pair with marinara sauce and sprinkle with grated cheese.

APPROXIMATE PREP TIME: 10-20 minutes

APPROXIMATE COOK TIME: 15-20 minutes

FRITTATA

SERVES 4

INGREDIENTS:

10 eggs
1/2 cup whole milk — *or light cream or non-dairy milk*
8 ounces shredded mozzarella — *or cheddar, provolone, or asiago*
1/4 cup grated Romano cheese
1/4 teaspoon ground black pepper
2 tablespoons extra virgin olive oil
4-6 ounces pancetta, sliced — *or bacon or prosciutto*
2 medium red bliss potatoes, cut into 1/2-inch pieces
1 small, sweet onion, diced
4 ounces roasted red peppers, thinly sliced — *or 2 plum tomatoes, diced*
8-10 ounces baby spinach

INSTRUCTIONS:

Pre-heat the oven to 350 degrees.

PREPARING THE MIXTURE:

In a large mixing bowl, combine the eggs, whole milk, shredded mozzarella, Romano cheese, and ground black pepper and whisk all ingredients thoroughly.

COOKING THE VEGETABLES:

In a large oven-safe skillet, add the extra virgin olive oil and bring to a medium heat. Next, add the potatoes and cook until golden brown, about 8-10 minutes, mix occasionally. Remove the potatoes from skillet and set aside. Continuing, on medium heat add the pancetta and cook until golden, about 3-4 minutes, mixing occasionally. Next, add the onion and roasted red peppers. Cook until the onions begin to soften, about 2-3 minutes, mixing occasionally. Next, add the cooked potatoes back into the skillet and the baby spinach, cook for 1 minute, mixing occasionally.

FRITTATA...CONTINUED

COOKING THE FRITTATA:

Continuing on medium heat, pour the egg mixture into the skillet, ensuring the vegetables are covered evenly. Next, cook the frittata until it begins to firm up and the egg begins to pull away from the sides of the skillet, about 5-7 minutes. Remove the skillet from the heat and bake in the oven until the frittata cooks through, about 10-15 minutes. Frittata should be firm and golden brown on top.

TO SERVE:

Place on serving dish or cut into squares and serve as an appetizer.

APPROXIMATE PREP TIME: 10-15 minutes

APPROXIMATE COOK TIME: 30-40 minutes

GREEN BEANS WITH TOMATOES AND GARLIC

SERVES 4

INGREDIENTS:

2-3 pounds green beans *(or 3 small zucchini, sliced or 20 ounces spinach)*

4 plum tomatoes, diced *(or 1 can (15-16 ounces) diced tomatoes)*

4 garlic cloves, sliced

1/2 cup extra virgin olive oil

1/2 teaspoon salt

1/2 teaspoon ground black pepper

INSTRUCTIONS:

PREPARING THE VEGETABLES:

Begin by removing the ends of the green beans and wash thoroughly.

COOKING THE VEGETABLES:

In a large pot, add in the extra virgin olive oil and bring to a high heat. Next, add in the garlic and sauté until golden, about 1-2 minutes. Lower to medium heat and add the green beans, salt, and ground black pepper. Sauté for 5 minutes, mixing occasionally. Next, add the tomatoes and sauté for 5 minutes, stirring occasionally to combine all ingredients, or until the green beans are tender.

TO SERVE:

Serve as a side dish with your favorite meat or seafood recipe. Alternatively, serve over pasta as a vegetarian option.

APPROXIMATE PREP TIME: 10-15 minutes

APPROXIMATE COOK TIME: 12-15 minutes

MACARONI SALAD

SERVES 8

INGREDIENTS:

2 pounds uncooked elbow pasta *(or shells)*
1/2 medium red onion, minced *(or sweet onion)*
2 medium carrots, shredded
2 stalks celery, minced *(or 1 teaspoon celery seed)*
1 cup mayonnaise
1/4 cup red wine vinegar *(or pickle juice)*
1/4 cup water
1/2 teaspoon salt
1/2 teaspoon garlic powder
1/2 teaspoon onion powder
1/4 teaspoon ground black pepper

INSTRUCTIONS:

COOKING THE PASTA:

Prepare the pasta according to the package instructions. Strain pasta and place in a large mixing bowl. Set aside to cool for 10 minutes.

PREPARING THE SALAD:

After pasta has cooled, add the remaining ingredients to the pasta. Mix ingredients well ensuring the mayonnaise is evenly spread and creamy.

TO SERVE:

Place the macaroni salad in a large serving bowl and serve as an appetizer or side dish. For best results, place the salad into the refrigerator for a least 4 hours before serving.

APPROXIMATE PREP TIME: 20-30 minutes
APPROXIMATE COOK TIME: 15-20 minutes

MOZZARELLA CAPRESE

SERVES 6

INGREDIENTS:

16 ounces fresh mozzarella, sliced
3 large tomatoes *(or 6 oz. sun-dried tomatoes or 6 oz. roasted red peppers)*
1/4 cup fresh basil, thinly sliced
2 tablespoons balsamic vinegar *(or red wine vinegar)*
1/4 cup extra virgin olive oil
1/2 teaspoon salt
1/4 teaspoon ground black pepper
1/4 teaspoon dried oregano

INSTRUCTIONS:

PREPARING THE CAPRESE:

Begin by slicing the fresh mozzarella and tomatoes ¼ inch thick. Ensure there are equal pieces of mozzarella and tomato. On a large plate, layer the mozzarella and tomatoes on top of each other forming a circle around the perimeter of the plate. When layering, ensure half of the mozzarella and tomato is exposed to the next layer (see page 35 for a visual aid). Layer any remaining mozzarella or tomatoes in the center of the circle.

DRESSING THE CAPRESE:

In a small bowl, add the balsamic vinegar, extra virgin olive oil, salt, ground black pepper, and oregano. Stir well to ensure all the ingredients are incorporated to form a dressing. Next, with a spoon, drizzle the dressing over the caprese salad as desired.

TO SERVE:

Serve this dish as an appetizer with Italian bread, or as a side dish with meat or seafood.

APPROXIMATE PREP TIME: 15-25 minutes

MOZZARELLA AND ROASTED RED PEPPER SALAD

SERVES 4

INGREDIENTS:

1 jar (16 ounces) roasted red pepper strips *(or sliced antipasto peppers)*
8 ounces fresh mozzarella balls *(or fresh mozzarella cut into 1/2 inch cubes)*
4 garlic cloves, thinly sliced
1/4 cup diced fresh parsley *(or sliced basil)*
1/4 cup of extra virgin olive oil
1/4 cup balsamic vinegar *(or red wine vinegar)*
1/4 teaspoon salt
Pinch ground black pepper

INSTRUCTIONS:

PREPARING THE SALAD:

In a large mixing bowl combine all ingredients and mix thoroughly.

TO SERVE:

Place mozzarella salad in a large serving bowl. For best results, place the salad into the refrigerator for a least 4 hours before serving. As a complementary pairing, serve with fresh toasted Italian bread.

APPROXIMATE PREP TIME: 10-15 minutes

MOZZARELLA AND TOMATO SALAD

SERVES 4

INGREDIENTS:

1 pint grape tomatoes *(or 8 ounces sun-dried tomatoes, sliced)*
8 ounces fresh mozzarella balls *(or fresh mozzarella cut into 1/2 inch cubes)*
1/2 cup extra virgin olive oil
1/2 cup red wine vinegar
1/4 cup diced fresh parsley *(or sliced basil)*
2 tablespoons balsamic vinegar
1/2 teaspoon salt
1/4 teaspoon ground black pepper

INSTRUCTIONS:

PREPARING THE SALAD:

In a large mixing bowl, combine all ingredients and mix thoroughly to incorporate.

TO SERVE:

Place mozzarella salad in a large serving bowl. For best results, place the salad into the refrigerator for a least 4 hours before serving. As a complementary pairing, serve with toasted Italian bread.

APPROXIMATE PREP TIME: 10-15 minutes

MOZZARELLA STICKS

SERVES 4

INGREDIENTS:

16 ounce mozzarella block
1 cup flour
4 eggs → or 1-2 cups buttermilk
1/2 cup water
2 cups plain breadcrumbs
1/2 teaspoon salt
1/2 teaspoon ground black pepper
1/2 teaspoon garlic powder
1/2 teaspoon onion powder
1-2 cups canola oil → or avocado oil or peanut oil

INSTRUCTIONS:

PREPARING THE MOZZARELLA:

Cut mozzarella into sticks about 3-inches long and ½-inch wide (or desired size) to form sticks. In a bowl, add the flour then dredge each mozzarella stick in flour and place on a baking sheet or plate to stage for breading.

BREADING THE MOZZARELLA:

In a mixing bowl, add the eggs and water and whisk to form an egg wash. Next, in another mixing bowl add the breadcrumbs, salt, ground black pepper, garlic powder, and onion powder, and mix thoroughly. Next, dredge each mozzarella stick in egg wash and then breadcrumbs. Repeat this process again to obtain a double-coat of breadcrumbs. Repeat the breading process until all the mozzarella sticks are double-coated with breadcrumbs.

MOZZARELLA STICKS...CONTINUED

COOKING THE MOZZARELLA STICKS:

In a large skillet, add the canola oil and bring to a high heat. Add in the mozzarella sticks, ensuring not to crowd the skillet, and cook each side until golden brown, about 1-2 minutes a side. Ensure you do not overcook the mozzarella sticks as the cheese will begin to break through the breading. Remove mozzarella sticks and strain on paper towel. Repeat this process until all the mozzarella sticks are cooked.

TO SERVE:

Serve as an appetizer or a side dish. Pair with marinara sauce and sprinkle with grated cheese.

APPROXIMATE PREP TIME: 20-30 minutes

APPROXIMATE COOK TIME: 15-20 minutes

POTATO CROQUETTES

SERVES 4

INGREDIENTS:

4 cups cooked mashed potatoes *(or sweet potatoes or instant potatoes)*

2 cups shredded mozzarella cheese *(or cheddar cheese or asiago cheese)*

1/2 cup grated Romano cheese

4-6 eggs

1/2 cup water

2 cups plain breadcrumbs

1/2 teaspoon salt

1/2 teaspoon garlic powder

1/4 teaspoon ground black pepper

1 cup flour

2-3 cups canola oil

INSTRUCTIONS:

PREPARING THE CROQUETTES:

In a large mixing bowl combine the cooked mashed potatoes, mozzarella, Romano cheese, and 2 eggs. Mix all ingredients well and place in the refrigerator to cool for 1 hour. Remove potato mixture from refrigerator and with your hands form croquettes by molding two tablespoons of the potato mixture into log shapes. Place formed croquettes into the freezer for 2 hours.

BREADING THE CROQUETTES:

In a mixing bowl, add in 4 eggs and the water and whisk to form an egg wash. In another bowl add the breadcrumbs, salt, ground black pepper, and garlic powder and mix well. In a third bowl, add the flour. Remove croquettes from the freezer and dredge croquettes in flour then place in egg wash and then breadcrumbs. Place in egg wash and breadcrumbs again to create a double-coat of breadcrumbs. Repeat this process until all of the croquettes are double-coated in breadcrumbs.

POTATO CROQUETTES...CONTINUED

COOKING THE CROQUETTES:

In a large skillet, add in 2 cups canola oil and bring to a high heat. Add in the croquettes, ensuring not to crowd the skillet, and cook each side until golden brown, about 2-3 minutes a side. Remove croquettes and strain on paper towel. Use more canola oil as needed. Repeat this process until all the croquettes are cooked.

TO SERVE:

Serve as an appetizer or a side dish. Pair with marinara sauce and sprinkle with grated cheese.

APPROXIMATE PREP TIME:	3 1/2 - 4 hours
APPROXIMATE COOK TIME:	20-30 minutes

POTATO SALAD

SERVES 8

INGREDIENTS:

3 pounds red bliss potatoes, cut into 1 x 1-inch pieces *(or Yukon gold potatoes)*

2 medium carrots, shredded or minced

2 stalks of celery, minced *(or 1 tsp. celery seed)*

1 small red onion, minced

1 cup mayonnaise

1/4 cup red wine vinegar *(or pickle juice)*

1/4 cup water

1/2 teaspoon salt

1/4 teaspoon ground black pepper

1/2 teaspoon garlic powder

1/2 teaspoon onion powder

INSTRUCTIONS:

COOKING THE POTATOES:

Begin by washing the potatoes and cutting the potatoes into 1 x 1-inch pieces. Next, add the potatoes into a large pot and cover with water until potatoes are floating. Place the large pot onto high heat and bring to a boil. Lower to a simmer and cook for 30 minutes or until potatoes are fork tender. Strain the potatoes and place in a large mixing bowl. Let the potatoes cool for 10 minutes.

PREPARING THE SALAD:

After the potatoes have cooled, add the remaining ingredients to the potatoes. Mix ingredients well ensuring the mayonnaise is evenly spread and creamy.

TO SERVE:

Place the potato salad in a large serving bowl and serve as an appetizer or as a side dish. For best results, refrigerate for at least 4 hours before serving.

APPROXIMATE PREP TIME: 20-30 minutes

APPROXIMATE COOK TIME: 40-45 minutes

Rotini Pasta Salad

ROTINI PASTA SALAD

SERVES 4

INGREDIENTS:

1 pound uncooked rotini pasta

1 jar (16 ounces) roasted red peppers, sliced *(or 8 ounces sun-dried tomatoes, sliced)*

1 can/jar (12 ounces) artichoke hearts (quartered)

1 can (6-8 ounces) sliced black olives

1/2 stick sweet, dried sausage cut into 1/4-inch cubes or thin sticks *(or pepperoni)*

1/2 cup of extra virgin olive oil

8 ounces fresh mozzarella cut into 1/4-inch cubes *(or sharp provolone)*

1/4 small red onion, sliced

1/4 cup diced fresh parsley

1/4 cup of red wine vinegar

2 tablespoons balsamic vinegar

1/2 teaspoon salt

1/4 teaspoon ground black pepper

1/4 teaspoon garlic powder

INSTRUCTIONS:

PREPARING THE PASTA:

Prepare the pasta according to package instructions. Strain pasta and place in a large mixing bowl. Set aside to cool for 10 minutes.

PREPARING THE SALAD:

Once the rotini has cooled, combine all ingredients, and mix thoroughly to incorporate.

TO SERVE:

Place the rotini pasta salad in a large serving bowl. For best results, refrigerate for at least 4 hours before serving.

APPROXIMATE PREP TIME: 20-25 minutes

APPROXIMATE COOK TIME: 15-20 minutes

SPINACH WITH TOMATOES AND EGGS

SERVES 2

INGREDIENTS:

1/2 cup extra virgin olive oil
4 garlic cloves, sliced
15-20 ounces fresh baby spinach — *or kale or Swiss chard*
1 cup chicken broth — *or vegetable broth*
1/2 teaspoon salt
1/4 teaspoon ground black pepper
1 can (15-16 ounces) diced tomatoes — *or 8 ounces roasted red peppers, sliced*
4 eggs

INSTRUCTIONS:

COOKING THE VEGETABLES:

In large pot, add in the extra virgin olive oil and bring to a high heat. Next, add in the garlic and sauté until golden, about 1-2 minutes. Lower to medium heat and add one half of the baby spinach, 1/2 cup of chicken broth, salt, and ground black pepper. Stir until leaves reduce by half, about 2-3 minutes, then add remaining baby spinach, 1/2 cup of chicken broth, and diced tomatoes. Bring to a simmer and cook for 2 minutes. Next, add the eggs and mix until eggs cook, ensuring the yolks break, about 2-3 minutes.

TO SERVE:

Serve as a side dish with your favorite meat or seafood recipe. For an alternative option, serve as a healthy breakfast.

APPROXIMATE PREP TIME: 5-10 minutes

APPROXIMATE COOK TIME: 10-15 minutes

Stuffed Artichokes

STUFFED ARTICHOKES

YIELDS 6

INGREDIENTS:

2 lemons cut into 12 wedges

6 medium artichokes

2 cups extra virgin olive oil

1 cup plain breadcrumbs

1/2 cup grated Romano cheese *(or Parmigiano Reggiano)*

2 tablespoons plus 1 teaspoon salt

1/4 teaspoon ground black pepper

2 garlic cloves, sliced

INSTRUCTIONS:

CLEANING THE ARTICHOKES:

Begin cleaning the artichokes by pulling away all small leaves from the stem and bottom of artichoke. Next, cut off the stem, ensuring the artichoke can sit flat in a pot. Next, cut away about 1/4 of an inch across the top of artichoke to reveal the inside and trim the remaining top leaves with a pair of scissors to remove all sharp edges. With thumbs, pull apart artichoke slightly to separate inside leaves. Next, peel away any remaining damaged outside leaves and place the artichokes in a pot of cold water with 6 lemon wedges (lemon helps with discoloring of artichokes). Repeat this process until all the artichokes are cleaned and placed into the lemon water.

PREPARING THE FILLING:

In medium skillet add in 1 cup of extra virgin olive oil and bring to a medium heat. Next, add in breadcrumbs and roast on medium heat, mixing occasionally, until breadcrumbs turn light brown in color, about 3-4 minutes. Remove from heat and place in small bowl to cool for 10 minutes. While cooling add grated cheese, 1 teaspoon salt, and ground black pepper and mix well.

STUFFED ARTICHOKES...CONTINUED

STUFFING THE ARTICHOKES:

Begin by removing the artichokes from the water and place in a colander. Follow this process for each artichoke:
- Place a few slices (3-4) of garlic inside artichoke
- Spread a teaspoonful of breadcrumbs throughout the artichoke leaves.
- Pour about 1 teaspoon of extra virgin olive oil on top of the artichoke to saturate the breadcrumbs.
- Add another teaspoonful of breadcrumbs to the top of artichoke and spread throughout.

Arrange the stuffed artichokes in a single layer at bottom of a large pot. If needed, add a little bit more extra virgin olive oil to the tops of the artichokes if the breadcrumbs look dry. Next, place remaining 6 lemon wedges and 2 tablespoons of salt to the bottom of the pot between artichokes. Add water to the pot until water level reaches the top of artichokes but does not cover them.

COOKING THE ARTICHOKES:

Place the pot with the artichokes on high heat until water comes to a boil. Lower to a simmer and cook until artichoke leaves are tender, about 30-40 minutes. Add water to the pot as needed to maintain the water level to the top of the artichokes.

TO SERVE:

Place the artichokes on a serving dish or large plate and serve as an appetizer or side dish. In my family, these artichokes are made for Thanksgiving or Christmas dinner as a side dish.

APPROXIMATE PREP TIME:	50-70 minutes
APPROXIMATE COOK TIME:	50-60 minutes

STUFFED MUSHROOMS

YIELDS 1 DOZEN

INGREDIENTS:

12 whole cremini mushrooms
1/4 cup extra virgin olive oil
3 garlic cloves, minced
1/2 cup breadcrumbs
1/4 cup grated Romano cheese *(or Parmigiano Reggiano)*
1/4 teaspoon salt
1/4 teaspoon ground black pepper
1/4 teaspoon onion powder *(or 1 small onion, minced)*

INSTRUCTIONS:

Pre-heat the oven to 350 degrees

PREPARING THE MUSHROOMS:

Rinse the mushrooms thoroughly in water. Remove the stems of the mushrooms with your fingers or a spoon. Make sure the caps of the mushrooms remain whole. Dice the stems of the mushrooms and set aside to add to the stuffing.

PREPARING THE STUFFING:

In large skillet, add in the extra virgin olive oil and bring to a high heat. Next, add in the garlic and sauté until golden, about 1-2 minutes. Next, lower the heat to medium, add in the mushroom stems, and sauté for 2 minutes. Next, add in the breadcrumbs, grated cheese, salt, pepper, and onion powder. Sauté for 5 minutes or until the breadcrumbs begin to toast, mixing occasionally. Remove the stuffing from the heat and set aside to cool.

COOKING THE MUSHROOMS:

Spoon in enough stuffing to fill each mushroom cap to the top. Place the mushrooms onto a baking sheet and bake at 350 degrees until the mushrooms are browned, about 30-40 minutes.

TO SERVE:

Place the stuffed mushrooms on a serving dish or large plate and serve as an appetizer or side dish.

APPROXIMATE PREP TIME: 15-20 minutes
APPROXIMATE COOK TIME: 40-50 minutes

STUFFED PEPPERS

YIELDS 6

INGREDIENTS:

1 cup white rice → *or brown rice, couscous, or quinoa*

2 tablespoons extra virgin olive oil

3 garlic cloves, minced

1 pound ground beef (80/20) → *or ground turkey, chicken, or pork*

6 bell peppers, any color

1/4 cup shredded mozzarella cheese → *or shredded asiago or shredded provolone*

INSTRUCTIONS:

Pre-heat the oven to 350 degrees

PREPARING THE RICE:

Cook the white rice according to package instructions.

PREPARING THE STUFFING:

In large skillet, add in the extra virgin olive oil and bring to a high heat. Next, add in the garlic and sauté until golden, about 1-2 minutes. Next, add the ground beef and cook on medium heat until browned, about 5-7 minutes, mixing occasionally. Strain the excess grease and return the skillet to medium heat. Add in the cooked rice, mozzarella cheese, and 1/2 cup of marinara sauce. Cook for 2 minutes and mix well to incorporate all the ingredients.

PREPARING THE PEPPERS:

Start by cutting the tops off the bell peppers and clean them out by removing the seeds. Next, spoon in enough stuffing to fill the peppers to the top. With a tablespoon, add a spoonful of marinara sauce to the top of the peppers. Place the peppers onto a baking pan and bake at 350 degrees until the peppers are browned, about 20-30 minutes.

TO SERVE:

Place the stuffed peppers on a serving dish or large plate and serve as an appetizer or side dish. As an alternative, feature the stuffed peppers as the main entrée for a healthy dinner option.

APPROXIMATE PREP TIME: 15-20 minutes
APPROXIMATE COOK TIME: 50-60 minutes

TOMATO AND CUCUMBER SALAD

SERVES 4

INGREDIENTS:

4 plum tomatoes, sliced — *or 4 ounces sun-dried tomatoes, sliced*

1 large or 2 small cucumbers, sliced

1 small red onion, sliced — *or sweet onion, sliced*

1/2 cup of extra virgin olive oil

1/2 cup of red wine vinegar

2 tablespoons balsamic vinegar

1/2 teaspoon salt

1/4 teaspoon ground black pepper

INSTRUCTIONS:

PREPARING THE SALAD:

In a large mixing bowl, combine all ingredients and mix thoroughly to incorporate.

TO SERVE:

Place tomato cucumber salad in a large serving bowl. For best results, refrigerate for at least 4 hours before serving.

APPROXIMATE PREP TIME: 15-20 minutes

TOMATO SOUP

SERVES 2

INGREDIENTS:

- 2 tablespoons extra virgin olive oil
- 4 garlic cloves, sliced
- 1 medium sweet onion, chopped *(or 1 red onion or 2 shallots)*
- 1 can (6 ounces) tomato paste
- 1/2 teaspoon dried oregano
- 1/2 teaspoon dried basil
- 1 teaspoon salt
- 1/2 teaspoon ground black pepper
- 2 cups vegetable broth *(or chicken broth or beef broth)*
- 1 can (28-35 ounces) crushed tomatoes *(or tomato puree)*
- 1 tablespoon sugar
- 1 can (15-16 ounces) cannellini beans (with liquid) *(or navy beans or kidney beans)*

INSTRUCTIONS:

PREPARING THE SOUP:

In a medium pot, add the extra virgin olive oil and bring to a high heat. Next, add in the garlic and sauté until golden, about 1-2 minutes. Next, add the onions and sauté for 2 minutes, mixing occasionally. Next, add the tomato paste, dried oregano, dried basil, salt, ground black pepper, and vegetable broth. Incorporate all ingredients by stirring occasionally and cooking for 5 minutes on medium heat. Next, add the crushed tomatoes and sugar. Bring to a simmer and cook for 30 minutes, stirring occasionally. Next, pour the soup into a blender and add in the beans. Blend well to form a creamy, smooth consistency.

TO SERVE:

Serve as a side dish or appetizer with a grilled cheese sandwich or toasted Italian bread.

APPROXIMATE PREP TIME: 15-20 minutes
APPROXIMATE COOK TIME: 45-50 minutes

Tortellini Salad

TORTELLINI SALAD

SERVES 4

INGREDIENTS:

1 package (19 ounces) tortellini
1 can (12 ounces) artichoke quarters — *or hearts of palm*
1/2 small red onion, thinly sliced
4 ounces sun-dried tomatoes, sliced — *or 4 ounces grape tomatoes*
4 ounces pitted kalamata olives, sliced — *or 4 ounces black sliced olives*
1/4 cup chopped fresh parsley
2 tablespoons extra virgin olive oil
2 tablespoons red wine vinegar
2 tablespoons balsamic vinegar
1/2 teaspoon salt
1/4 teaspoon ground black pepper
1/4 teaspoon garlic powder — *or 2 garlic cloves, minced*

INSTRUCTIONS:

PREPARING THE TORTELLINI:

Prepare the tortellini according to the package instructions. Strain the tortellini, place in a large mixing bowl, and set aside for 10 minutes to cool.

PREPARING THE SALAD:

Once tortellini have cooled, combine the remaining ingredients with the tortellini and mix thoroughly to incorporate.

TO SERVE:

Place tortellini salad in a large serving bowl. For best results, refrigerate for at least 4 hours before serving.

APPROXIMATE PREP TIME: 25-30 minutes
APPROXIMATE COOK TIME: 15-20 minutes

Zucchini and Tomatoes

ZUCCHINI AND TOMATOES

SERVES 4

INGREDIENTS:

3 medium zucchini, thinly sliced — or 2 eggplant or 1 cauliflower

1 can (15-16 ounces) diced tomatoes — or 2 plum tomatoes, diced

1 sweet onion, sliced — or 1 red onion, sliced

4 garlic cloves, sliced

1/4 cup extra virgin olive oil

1/2 teaspoon salt

1/2 teaspoon ground black pepper

INSTRUCTIONS:

PREPARING THE ZUCCHINI:

In a large skillet, add the extra virgin olive oil and bring to a high heat. Next, add the garlic and sauté until golden, about 1-2 minutes. Lower to medium heat, add in the onion, and sauté for 2 minutes, mixing occasionally. Next, add in the zucchini, salt, and ground black pepper and sauté for 5 minutes, mixing occasionally. Finally, add in the diced tomatoes and sauté until the zucchini is tender, about 5-8 minutes, mixing occasionally.

TO SERVE:

Serve the zucchini as a side dish or feature with pasta for a main entrée.

APPROXIMATE PREP TIME: 10 minutes

APPROXIMATE COOK TIME: 20-30 minutes

PASTA

INTRODUCTION TO PASTA

Pasta! Pasta! Pasta! I love pasta! I could eat pasta every day, and even many times a day. Pasta is so versatile. It works with so many combinations of ingredients and can even stand on its own as the main feature in a dish.

Two of these pasta recipes, baked ziti and lasagna, are staple Italian American dishes. Baked ziti and lasagna are such great comfort foods, and they remind me of Sunday dinners growing up. One of the great things about these dishes is you can prepare them a day or two in advance and refrigerate, or even as early as the week before and freeze them until you are ready to cook.

I make pasta aglio e olio (garlic and oil) several times a month. It is a great weeknight meal, especially when I am looking for comfort food. From time to time, I will add broccoli or green beans to the pasta aglio e olio. This is a great way to incorporate some healthy vegetables.

The creamy pasta and broccoli recipe is super simple to prepare. With only four ingredients, the preparation time is short. The creaminess of the cheese is balanced well with the savory marinara sauce. The healthy addition of broccoli rounds out the dish.

With the overabundance of vegetables from my garden, pasta primavera is a favorite dish of mine to make in the summer. The freshness of the vegetables and comfort of the pasta are a fantastic combination.

Some other favorite recipes in this section are pasta e fagioli, rigatoni and broccoli rabe, and spaghetti Bolognese. Pick a few of your favorite pasta recipes, give them a try, and then invent the recipe that works the best for you.

BAKED ZITI

SERVES 4

INGREDIENTS:

2 pounds uncooked ziti
2 pounds ground beef — *or ground turkey, chicken, or pork*
6 cups marinara sauce — *or vodka sauce*
2 pounds ricotta cheese
1/2 cup Romano cheese — *or Parmigiano Reggiano*
4 cups shredded mozzarella cheese

INSTRUCTIONS:

Pre-heat the oven to 375 degrees.

COOKING THE ZITI:

Prepare the ziti according to the package instructions for al dente pasta. Strain ziti and let sit for 10 minutes.

COOKING THE GROUND BEEF:

While the ziti is cooking, place a large skillet on high heat and add the 2 pounds of ground beef. Cook for 8-10 minutes, until no longer pink, while mixing frequently to break up the ground beef and to cook evenly. Strain the grease and set the ground beef aside.

PREPARING THE ZITI MIXTURE:

In large mixing bowl, add the cooked ziti, 4 cups of marinara sauce, 2 pounds of ricotta cheese, 1/2 cup of Romano cheese, 2 cups of mozzarella cheese, and ground beef. Fold the mixture with a large spoon until all ingredients are well incorporated.

BAKED ZITI...CONTINUED

BRINGING EVERYTHING TOGETHER:

To a 9 x 13-inch baking dish, add 1 cup of marinara sauce and spread evenly on the bottom. Next, add ziti mixture to the baking dish and spread evenly. Next, add 1 cup of marinara sauce to the top of the ziti and spread evenly. Next, spread the 2 cups of mozzarella cheese evenly to cover the ziti. Finally, cover the ziti with aluminum foil and bake on 375 degrees for 30 minutes. Uncover the ziti and bake for another 10 minutes until the cheese is golden brown. Remove from the oven and let the baked ziti rest for 10 minutes before serving.

TO SERVE:

Cut the baked ziti into squares and serve with additional marinara sauce and grated cheese over top.

APPROXIMATE PREP TIME:	20-25 minutes
APPROXIMATE COOK TIME:	60-70 minutes

CACIO E PEPE (Cheese and Pepper)

SERVES 4

INGREDIENTS:

1 pound of uncooked spaghetti

1/4 cup extra virgin olive oil *(or 4 tablespoons unsalted butter)*

2 cups starchy water from cooked spaghetti

1 teaspoon coarse (fresh ground) black pepper, plus more for serving

3/4 cup grated Romano cheese, plus more for serving *(or finely shredded asiago)*

INSTRUCTIONS:

PREPARING THE PASTA:

Prepare the spaghetti according to the package instructions for al dente pasta. Before straining the spaghetti, remove 2 cups of starchy water and set aside.

BRINGING EVERYTHING TOGETHER:

While spaghetti is cooking, place a large skillet on medium heat and add 1/2 cup of extra virgin olive oil. Next, add the ground black pepper and cook for 1 minute, mixing occasionally. Next, turn off the heat to the skillet, add in the starchy water, and stir well to incorporate. With the heat still turned off, add in the Romano cheese and stir well to incorporate. Turn the heat to medium and stir the sauce constantly until the cheese is melted and the sauce is smooth and creamy, about 2-3 minutes. Finally, add in the cooked spaghetti and cook for 2 minutes, mixing occasionally.

TO SERVE:

Place pasta in a large serving bowl. Add more fresh ground pepper or Romano cheese to taste.

APPROXIMATE PREP TIME:	5 minutes
APPROXIMATE COOK TIME:	20-25 minutes

CAVATELLI AND BROCCOLI

SERVES 4

INGREDIENTS:

- 1 pound of uncooked cavatelli *(or ziti, penne, or gemelli)*
- 1/2 cup extra virgin olive oil *(or 1/2 stick unsalted butter)*
- 6 garlic cloves, thinly sliced
- 4 cups broccoli florets *(or 2 bunches broccoli rabe)*
- 1 cup chicken broth *(or vegetable broth)*
- 1/2 teaspoon salt
- 1/4 teaspoon ground black pepper
- 1/4 cup chopped fresh parsley
- Grated Romano cheese to serve

INSTRUCTIONS:

PREPARING THE PASTA:

Prepare the cavatelli according to the package instructions for al dente pasta. Strain pasta and set aside.

BRINGING EVERYTHING TOGETHER:

While the cavatelli is cooking, in a large skillet or pot, add the extra virgin olive oil and bring to a high heat. Next, add the garlic and sauté until golden, about 1-2 minutes. Reduce to medium heat and add the broccoli florets and sauté for 4 minutes, mixing occasionally. Next, add the chicken broth, salt, ground black pepper, and fresh parsley. Bring to a simmer and cook for 5 minutes, mixing occasionally. Finally, add in the cooked cavatelli and cook for 4 minutes, mixing occasionally, or until the broccoli is tender.

TO SERVE:

Place pasta in a large serving bowl, spoon sauce over, and sprinkle with grated cheese to taste.

APPROXIMATE PREP TIME: 10-15 minutes

APPROXIMATE COOK TIME: 25-35 minutes

Creamy Pasta and Broccoli

CREAMY PASTA AND BROCCOLI

SERVES 4

INGREDIENTS:

1 pound rigatoni — or ziti, penne, or gemelli

2 cups broccoli florets — or 12 ounces frozen peas or 20 ounces fresh spinach

8-12 ounces marinara sauce

1 cup ricotta cheese — or cottage cheese

INSTRUCTIONS:

PREPARING THE RIGATONI:

Prepare the rigatoni according to the instructions on the package for al dente pasta. Strain the rigatoni and return to the pot.

PREPARING THE BROCCOLI:

While the rigatoni is cooling, in a separate pot, add in the broccoli and cover half-way with water. Bring to a boil and cook for 5 minutes. Remove the broccoli from the water and set aside.

BRINGING EVERYTHING TOGETHER:

Place the pot with rigatoni on medium heat and add in the broccoli, marinara sauce, and ricotta cheese. Mix well to incorporate all the ingredients. Cook for about 5 minutes, mixing occasionally, or until the broccoli is tender and all the ingredients are hot and the sauce is creamy. If desired, add more marinara sauce for a less creamy sauce.

TO SERVE:

Place the pasta in a large serving dish and add more marinara sauce if desired. Pair with toasted Italian bread.

APPROXIMATE PREP TIME: 5-10 minutes

APPROXIMATE COOK TIME: 20-25 minutes

Farfalle with Sausage and Broccoli

FARFALLE WITH SAUSAGE AND BROCCOLI

SERVES 4

INGREDIENTS:

1 pound farfalle

4 sweet Italian sausage links *(or chicken sausage or turkey sausage)*

2 tablespoons extra virgin olive oil

4 garlic cloves, sliced

1 sweet onion, sliced

2 cups broccoli florets *(or green beans or asparagus)*

1/2 cup vegetable broth *(or chicken broth or pasta water)*

1/2 teaspoon salt

1/2 teaspoon crushed red pepper flakes

Grated Romano cheese to serve

INSTRUCTIONS:

PREPARING THE FARFALLE:

Prepare the farfalle according to the instructions on the package for al dente pasta. Strain farfalle and set aside.

PREPARING THE SAUSAGE:

While the farfalle is cooking, remove the sausage from the casings. Next, in a large skillet, add the extra virgin olive oil and bring to a high heat. Next, add the garlic and sauté until golden, about 1-2 minutes. Reduce to medium heat and add in the onion and sauté for 2 minutes, mixing occasionally. Next, add in the sausage and sauté for 5 minutes, while mixing thoroughly and breaking up the sausage.

FARFALLE WITH SAUSAGE AND BROCCOLI...CONTINUED

BRINGING EVERYTHING TOGETHER:

Continuing on medium heat, add in the broccoli, vegetable stock, and salt and bring to a simmer, and cook for 5 minutes, mixing occasionally. Finally, add in the cooked farfalle and red pepper flakes and cook for 2 minutes, mixing occasionally to incorporate all the ingredients, or until the broccoli is tender.

TO SERVE:

Place the farfalle with sausage and broccoli in a large serving bowl and sprinkle with grated cheese.

APPROXIMATE PREP TIME: 10-15 minutes

APPROXIMATE COOK TIME: 35-45 minutes

GNOCCHI MARINARA

SERVES 2

INGREDIENTS:

1 package of gnocchi *(or ravioli or tortellini)*

24 ounces marinara sauce *(or vodka sauce)*

1/4 cup grated Romano cheese, plus more to serve

INSTRUCTIONS:

PREPARING THE GNOCCHI:

Prepare the gnocchi according to the package instructions. Strain gnocchi and set aside.

BRINGING EVERYTHING TOGETHER:

Place 24 ounces of marinara sauce in a large pot on medium heat and bring to a simmer. Add in cooked gnocchi and grated cheese and mix thoroughly to incorporate. Cook for 5 minutes, mixing occasionally, or until the gnocchi is to your desired temperature.

TO SERVE:

Sprinkle the gnocchi with grated cheese and serve as a side or main dish.

APPROXIMATE PREP TIME:	5 minutes
APPROXIMATE COOK TIME:	20-25 minutes

Lasagna with Meat

LASAGNA WITH MEAT

SERVES 8

INGREDIENTS:

2 pounds uncooked lasagna noodles
1 pound of 80/20 ground beef *(or ground turkey, chicken, or pork)*
1/2 teaspoon salt
1/4 teaspoon ground black pepper
1/2 teaspoon garlic powder
2 pounds of ricotta cheese
3 cups of shredded mozzarella cheese *(or shredded asiago)*
1 cup of grated Romano cheese, plus more to serve
4 cups of marinara sauce, plus more to serve *(or vodka sauce)*

INSTRUCTIONS:

Pre-heat the oven to 350 degrees.

PREPARING THE PASTA:

Prepare the lasagna according to the package instructions for al dente pasta. Be sure to stir occasionally to prevent the lasagna noodles from sticking together. Strain pasta and rinse with cold water. Place noodles on wax paper for easy assembly of the lasagna.

PREPARING THE GROUND BEEF:

While the lasagna noodles are cooking, in a large skillet on high heat, add the ground beef, salt, ground black pepper, and garlic powder. Cook until ground beef is no longer pink, about 5-7 minutes, stirring occasionally. Remove ground beef to a bowl to cool.

PREPARING THE CHEESE MIXTURE:

In a large bowl combine the ricotta cheese, 2 cups of mozzarella cheese, and 1/2 cup of grated Romano cheese. Reserve 1 cup of mozzarella cheese and ½ cup of grated cheese for the top of the lasagna.

LASAGNA WITH MEAT...CONTINUED

BUILDING THE LASAGNA:

In the bottom of a 9 x 13-inch baking pan add 1 cup of marinara sauce and spread evenly. Next, place enough lasagna noodles (about 6) on top of the marinara sauce to completely cover the bottom of the pan. Next, spoon in half of the cheese mixture and spread evenly over the lasagna noodles. Then add in half of the ground beef and spread evenly over the cheese mixture. Next, add in 1 cup of marinara sauce and spread evenly over the ground beef.

Next, repeat this process to complete a second layer consisting of lasagna noodles, cheese mixture, ground beef, and marinara sauce.

To finish building the lasagna, place enough lasagna noodles (about 6) on top of the second layer of lasagna. Then, spread 1 cup of marinara sauce evenly over the noodles. Finally, spread 1 cup of mozzarella cheese over the marinara sauce and sprinkle 1/2 cup of grated Romano cheese to finish.

COOKING THE LASAGNA:

Cover the lasagna with aluminum foil and bake for 40 minutes. Uncover the lasagna and bake for 10 minutes, or until the cheese is melted and golden brown. Remove the lasagna from the oven and let rest for 10 minutes before serving.

TO SERVE:

Cut the lasagna into squares and serve with additional marinara sauce and grated cheese, as desired.

APPROXIMATE PREP TIME:	20-30 minutes
APPROXIMATE COOK TIME:	80-90 minutes

PASTA AGLIO E OLIO

SERVES 4

INGREDIENTS:

1 pound of uncooked spaghetti — *or your favorite pasta*

1/2 cup extra virgin olive oil

10 garlic cloves, thinly sliced

1 cup vegetable broth — *or chicken broth or pasta water*

1/2 teaspoon salt

1/4 cup chopped fresh parlsey

2 tablespoons grated Romano cheese, plus more to serve

1/2 teaspoon of crushed red pepper, plus more to serve

INSTRUCTIONS:

PREPARING THE PASTA:

Prepare the spaghetti according to the package instructions for al dente pasta. Strain the spaghetti and set aside.

BRINGING EVERYTHING TOGETHER:

In a large skillet or pot, add the extra virgin olive oil and bring to a high heat. Next, add the garlic and sauté garlic until golden, about 1-2 minutes. Reduce to medium heat and add in the vegetable broth, salt, fresh parsley, and Romano cheese, bring to a simmer, and cook for 1 minute. Next, add in the cooked spaghetti and crushed red pepper and cook for 5 minutes, mixing occasionally.

TO SERVE:

Place pasta in a large serving bowl. Add more Romano cheese and crushed red pepper to taste.

APPROXIMATE PREP TIME: 10-15 minutes

APPROXIMATE COOK TIME: 20-30 minutes

Pasta e Fagioli

PASTA E FAGIOLI

SERVES 4

INGREDIENTS:

- 4 tablespoons unsalted butter *(or 1/4 cup olive oil)*
- 4 garlic cloves, sliced
- 1/4 cup diced pancetta *(or bacon, prosciutto, or ham)*
- 1 medium sweet onion, diced
- 1 medium carrot, shredded
- 1 can (15-16 ounces) cannellini beans (with liquid) *(or navy beans or great northern beans)*
- 1 can (15-16 ounces) diced tomatoes
- 1/2 teaspoon salt
- 1/2 teaspoon ground black pepper
- 8 ounces ditalini pasta
- 4 cups chicken broth *(or vegetable broth)*
- 1 can (6 ounces) tomato paste
- 1/4 cup grated Romano cheese, plus more to serve

INSTRUCTIONS:

PREPARING THE PASTA E FAGIOLI:

In a large pot, add in the unsalted butter and melt on medium heat. Next, add in the garlic and pancetta and sauté for 2 minutes, mixing occasionally. Next, add in the onions and carrots and sauté for 2 minutes, mixing occasionally. Next, add in the beans, diced tomatoes, salt, and ground black pepper. Bring to a simmer and cook for 4 minutes, mixing occasionally. Next, add in the pasta, chicken stock, and tomato paste and mix until the tomato paste incorporates. Bring to a simmer and cook for 10-15 minutes, or until the pasta is to the desired consistency. Before serving, add in the grated cheese and mix well.

TO SERVE:

Place in a large serving bowl and sprinkle with grated cheese. Serve with toasted Italian bread.

APPROXIMATE PREP TIME: 15-20 minutes
APPROXIMATE COOK TIME: 25-30 minutes

PASTA PRIMAVERA

SERVES 4

INGREDIENTS:

2 zucchini, cut into thin strips

2 yellow squash, cut into thin strips — *or 1 large eggplant*

2 carrots, cut into 1-inch long thin strips

2 red bell peppers, cut into thin strips

1 sweet onion, sliced

1/2 cup sun-dried tomatoes, cut into strips — *or 2 plum tomatoes quartered*

6 garlic cloves, peeled

1 pound uncooked farfalle — *or penne, rigatoni, or gemelli*

1/2 cup extra virgin olive oil

1 teaspoon salt

1/2 teaspoon ground black pepper

1/2 cup Romano cheese, plus more to serve

INSTRUCTIONS:

Pre-heat the oven to 425 degrees.

PREPARING THE VEGETABLES:

On a large baking sheet, add the zucchini, yellow squash, carrots, red bell peppers, onion, sun-dried tomatoes, garlic, extra virgin olive oil, salt, and ground black pepper and mix well. After mixing, ensure the vegetables are spread out evenly on the baking sheet. Roast for 30 minutes, mixing the vegetables halfway through.

PREPARING THE PASTA:

While the vegetables are roasting, in a large pot, prepare the farfalle according to the package instructions for al dente pasta. Strain the pasta and return the pasta to the pot on low heat.

PASTA PRIMAVERA...CONTINUED

BRINGING EVERYTHING TOGETHER:

Add the Romano cheese and roasted vegetables to the hot pasta, ensuring the liquid from the vegetables is added as well. Cook for 2 minutes, mixing occasionally.

TO SERVE:

Place pasta in a large serving bowl and sprinkle more Romano cheese, if desired.

APPROXIMATE PREP TIME: 20-30 minutes
APPROXIMATE COOK TIME: 50-55 minutes

PENNE A LA VODKA

SERVES 4

INGREDIENTS:

1 pound uncooked penne *(or ziti, rigatoni, or gemelli)*

24 ounces vodka sauce

1/2 cup grated Romano cheese, plus more to serve

INSTRUCTIONS:

PREPARING THE PASTA:

Prepare the penne according to the package instructions for al dente pasta. Strain penne and set aside.

PREPARING THE A LA VODKA:

On medium heat, place 24 ounces of vodka sauce in a large pot and bring to a simmer. Add in the cooked penne and grated cheese and mix thoroughly to incorporate. Cook for 5 minutes, mixing occasionally, or until the pasta is to your desired temperature.

TO SERVE:

Place pasta in a large serving bowl and pour remaining sauce over. Sprinkle additional grated cheese over the pasta if desired.

APPROXIMATE PREP TIME: 5 minutes

APPROXIMATE COOK TIME: 25-35 minutes

RIGATONI AND BROCCOLI RABE

SERVES 4

INGREDIENTS:

1 pound rigatoni — *or penne, ziti, or gemelli*

2 bunches broccoli rabe — *or 20 ounces spinach, or 2 bunches Swiss chard*

1/2 cup extra virgin olive oil

5 garlic cloves, thinly sliced

1 cup chicken broth — *or vegetable broth or pasta water*

1/2 teaspoon salt

1/4 teaspoon ground black pepper

Crushed red pepper to taste

INSTRUCTIONS:

PREPARING THE PASTA:

Prepare the rigatoni according to the package instructions for al dente pasta. Strain rigatoni and set aside.

BRINGING EVERYTHING TOGETHER:

While the rigatoni is cooking, remove the bottom third portion of each broccoli rabe stem. In a large pot, add in the extra virgin olive oil and bring to a high heat. Next, add in the garlic and sauté until golden, about 1-2 minutes. Reduce to medium heat and add in the broccoli rabe and sauté for 5 minutes, mixing occasionally. Next, add chicken broth, salt, and ground black pepper. Bring to a simmer and cook for 5 minutes, mixing occasionally. Next add in the cooked rigatoni, red pepper flakes, and continue to simmer for 3 minutes, mixing occasionally to incorporate all ingredients.

TO SERVE:

Combine pasta and broccoli rabe in a large serving bowl and serve with crusty Italian bread.

APPROXIMATE PREP TIME: 10-15 minutes

APPROXIMATE COOK TIME: 35-40 minutes

SPAGHETTI BOLOGNESE

SERVES 4

INGREDIENTS:

1 pound ground beef (80/20) — *or ground turkey, chicken, or pork*

1 stick of unsalted butter

4 garlic cloves, sliced

1 can (28-35 ounces) crushed tomatoes

1/4 cup grated Romano cheese, plus more to serve

1 teaspoon dried oregano

1/2 teaspoon salt

1/4 teaspoon ground black pepper

1 pound spaghetti — *or linguini or fettucine*

INSTRUCTIONS:

PREPARING THE GROUND BEEF:

In a large skillet on high heat, add in the ground beef. Cook until ground beef is no longer pink, about 5-7 minutes, mixing occasionally while breaking up the beef. Once fully cooked, move ground beef to a bowl.

PREPARING THE SAUCE:

In a medium sauce pot, add in the unsalted butter and melt on medium heat. Next, add in the garlic and sauté until golden, about 1-2 minutes. Next, add in the crushed tomatoes, grated cheese, oregano, salt, and ground black pepper, bring to a simmer and cook for 20 minutes. Next, add in the cooked ground beef and continue to simmer for 10 minutes, mixing occasionally.

SPAGHETTI BOLOGNESE...CONTINUED

PREPARING THE PASTA:

While the sauce is cooking, in a large pot, prepare the spaghetti according to the package instructions for al dente pasta. Strain the pasta and return to the pot.

BRINGING EVERYTHING TOGETHER:

In the large pot add the Bolognese sauce to the spaghetti and mix thoroughly to incorporate. On medium heat, cook the spaghetti for 5 minutes, mixing occasionally, or until the spaghetti has reached the desired temperature.

TO SERVE:

Place in a large serving bowl and sprinkle with grated cheese.

APPROXIMATE PREP TIME:	10-15 minutes
APPROXIMATE COOK TIME:	65-75 minutes

SPAGHETTI WITH PEPPERS AND ONIONS

SERVES 4

INGREDIENTS:

1 pound spaghetti *(or linguini or fettucine)*

1/4 cup extra virgin olive oil

6 garlic cloves, sliced

2 sweet onions, sliced *(or red onions)*

4 bell peppers, any color, cut into thin strips

1 can (15-16 ounces) diced tomatoes *(or 3 plum tomatoes, diced)*

1/2 teaspoon salt

1/4 teaspoon ground black pepper

2 tablespoons Romano cheese, plus more to serve

INSTRUCTIONS:

PREPARING THE PASTA:

Prepare the spaghetti according to the package instructions for al dente pasta. Strain pasta and set aside.

PREPARING THE VEGETABLES:

While the spaghetti is cooking, in a large pot or skillet, add the extra virgin olive oil and bring to a high heat. Next, add the garlic and sauté until golden, about 1-2 minutes. Next, add the bell peppers, sweet onions, diced tomatoes, salt, and ground black pepper to the skillet. Sauté until the vegetables are tender, about 5-7 minutes, mixing occasionally.

BRINGING EVERYTHING TOGETHER:

Add the spaghetti and grated cheese to the vegetables and mix well. Cook for 2-3 minutes, or until the spaghetti reaches your desired temperature.

TO SERVE:

Place pasta in a large serving bowl and sprinkle with more Romano cheese if desired.

APPROXIMATE PREP TIME: 15-25 minutes

APPROXIMATE COOK TIME: 30-40 minutes

TORTELLINI AND PEAS

SERVES 4

INGREDIENTS:

2 tablespoons extra virgin olive oil
2 garlic cloves, minced
1 small, sweet onion, diced
1/2 teaspoon of salt
1/4 teaspoon ground black pepper
1 can (28-35 ounces) crushed tomatoes *or tomato puree*
1 package (12-16 ounces) frozen peas
1 package of tortellini *or your favorite pasta*
Grated Romano cheese to taste, plus more to serve

INSTRUCTIONS:

PREPARING THE SAUCE:

In a medium saucepan, bring the extra virgin olive oil to high heat. Next, add in the garlic and sauté until golden, about 1-2 minutes. Next, add in the onions, salt, and ground black pepper and sauté for 4 minutes, mixing occasionally. Next, add in the tomatoes and bring to a simmer, then cook for 20 minutes, mixing occasionally. Next, add in the frozen peas, bring the sauce to a simmer, and cook for 10 minutes, mixing occasionally.

PREPARING THE TORTELLINI:

While the sauce is simmering prepare the tortellini according to the instructions. Strain the tortellini and proceed to serve.

TO SERVE:

Place the cooked tortellini in the center of a bowl and spoon over the desired amount of sauce. Finish with a sprinkle of grated cheese to taste.

APPROXIMATE PREP TIME: 10-15 minutes
APPROXIMATE COOK TIME: 55-65 minutes

EGGPLANT

INTRODUCTION TO EGGPLANT

Welcome to the eggplant recipe section of the cookbook. Eggplant is one of my favorite vegetables and has been a staple in my family for as long as I can remember. My Nonno (grandpa) would go out to the garden in the morning, pick a few beautiful eggplants, and give them to my Nonna to cook. She would fry up some eggplant slices in good olive oil and layer the eggplant in a baking dish with fresh basil and grated parmesan cheese. This dish always makes me think about my family every time I prepare it.

My favorite eggplant dish to make is eggplant rollatini. When I was 16 years old, I worked in the Italian deli. Their eggplant rollatini was bought frozen. It was already filled with ricotta cheese, breaded, and fried. I felt that this was not what the customer was expecting from a homemade Italian deli. So, one Sunday morning, I asked the owner if I could try making the eggplant rollatini from scratch.

After some convincing he gave me the go ahead and I jumped right in. I had seen my Mom make fried eggplant before. So I started there with peeling the eggplant. Then, thinly slicing the eggplant on the deli slicer. Next, I breaded the eggplant, and then fried it in the deep fryer. Now that I had the eggplant fried, I needed to figure out the filling. Again I used my family as inspiration. I thought about my Mom's and Nonna's baked ziti and lasagna and went from there. I mixed together ricotta cheese, grated cheese, shredded mozzarella, and a few other ingredients. Next, I spread some filling on to the eggplant slices. I rolled the slices up, added some marinara sauce, and baked them in the oven.

The deli owner loved the rollatini and asked me to show him what I did. The following Sunday when I returned to work, I was greeted with four cases of eggplants! The owner said, "This is what you are doing today. Everything you need is in the walk-in refrigerator." I went to work and never looked back. Now, many years later, eggplant rollatini is my favorite dish to make and is the dish I will most often bring to a party.

The eggplant rollatini takes some time to prepare, but the payoff is well worth it!

Another fun recipe to prepare are the eggplant stacks. This is a unique recipe and is great as an appetizer, side dish, or main entrée. This recipe is distinctive and delicious. It will be a great conversation starter if you bring the eggplant stacks to a party.

EGGPLANT CASSEROLE (Sicilian Style)

SERVES 8

INGREDIENTS:

2 large eggplants *(or 4 zucchini)*

4 large eggs

1/2 cup water

2-3 cups plain breadcrumbs

1/2 teaspoon salt

1/4 teaspoon ground black pepper

2-3 cups canola oil

2-3 cups marinara sauce *(or vodka sauce)*

1 cup grated Romano cheese

2 cups chopped fresh basil

9 x 13-inch baking pan

INSTRUCTIONS:

Pre-heat the oven to 375 degrees.

PREPARING THE EGGPLANT:

Begin by cutting the ends off the eggplants and remove all the skin. Lay eggplant on its side and cut 1/4-inch thick slices, forming flat ovals, ensuring not to cut slices larger than 1/4-inch thick.

BREADING THE EGGPLANT:

In a large mixing bowl, add the eggs and water and whisk to form an egg wash. In another mixing bowl add 2 cups of breadcrumbs, salt and ground black pepper and mix well. Dredge each eggplant slice in the egg wash and then the breadcrumbs and place on a baking sheet to stage for cooking. Use the additional cup of breadcrumbs as needed.

EGGPLANT CASSEROLE...CONTINUED

FRYING THE EGGPLANT:

In a large skillet, add 2 cups of canola oil and bring to a high heat. Next, place 3-4 slices of eggplant into hot oil. Once the bottom of the eggplant slice begins to brown, about 1-2 minutes, flip it and brown the other side, about 1-2 minutes. Move eggplant slices to a baking sheet and stack between layers of paper towels to strain excess oil. Repeat this process until all eggplant slices have been cooked. Set aside and let the eggplant cool for 10 minutes.

LAYERING THE EGGPLANT:

On the bottom of a 9 x 13-inch baking pan, place one cup of marinara sauce and spread evenly. Next, cover the bottom of the pan with a layer of eggplant. Spoon about 1/2 cup of marinara sauce evenly over the eggplant. Next, sprinkle ¼ cup of grated cheese and a pinch of fresh basil on top of the sauce. Repeat this process until the pan is full or until all the eggplant has been used. For the top layer add additional grated cheese if desired.

BAKING THE EGGPLANT:

Cover the pan with aluminum foil and bake for 30 minutes. Remove foil and bake for an additional 10 minutes. Remove the eggplant from the oven and let rest for 5 minutes before serving.

TO SERVE:

Serve the eggplant casserole with a side of your favorite pasta or a small salad and Italian bread.

APPROXIMATE PREP TIME:	50-60 minutes
APPROXIMATE COOK TIME:	70-80 minutes

EGGPLANT GEMELLI

SERVES 4

INGREDIENTS:

1 eggplant

1/2 cup extra virgin olive oil, divided

1 teaspoon salt, divided

1/2 teaspoon ground black pepper, divided

1 pound gemelli pasta → *or your favorite pasta*

4 garlic cloves, sliced

1 can (15-16 ounces) diced tomatoes → *or 8 ounces sun-dried tomatoes, sliced*

1/4 cup fresh basil, sliced

1/2 cup ricotta cheese

Grated Romano cheese to serve

INSTRUCTIONS:

Pre-heat the oven to 400 degrees.

PREPARING THE EGGPLANT:

Begin by cutting the ends off the eggplant and removing the skin. Next, slice the eggplant in 1/4-inch thick slices and place on a baking sheet. Next, drizzle 1/4 cup of extra virgin olive oil evenly over the eggplant. Finally, sprinkle 1/2 teaspoon salt and 1/4 teaspoon ground black pepper evenly over the eggplant and bake in the oven for 15 minutes, or until the eggplant is golden. Remove the eggplant from the oven, cut into 1-inch thick strips, and set aside.

PREPARING THE PASTA:

While the eggplant is baking, prepare the gemelli pasta according to the package instructions for al dente pasta. Strain the pasta and set aside.

EGGPLANT GEMELLI...CONTINUED

BRINGING EVERYTHING TOGETHER:

In a large skillet add 1/4 cup of extra virgin olive oil and bring to a high heat. Next, add the garlic and sauté until golden, about 1-2 minutes. Reduce to medium heat and add in the diced tomatoes, fresh basil, 1/2 teaspoon salt, and 1/4 teaspoon of ground black pepper. Bring to a simmer and cook for 5 minutes, mixing occasionally. Continuing on medium heat, add in the cooked eggplant and cooked pasta and mix to incorporate everything. Cook for 5 minutes, mixing occasionally, or until the pasta has reached the desired temperature. Finally, remove the pasta mixture from the heat and add in the ricotta cheese and mix to incorporate everything.

TO SERVE:

Place in a large serving dish and sprinkle with grated cheese. Serve with Italian bread.

APPROXIMATE PREP TIME: 10-15 minutes

APPROXIMATE COOK TIME: 50-60 minutes

EGGPLANT PARMIGIANA

SERVES 8

INGREDIENTS:

2 large eggplants — *or 4 zucchini*
4 large eggs
1/2 cup water
2-3 cups plain breadcrumbs
1/2 teaspoon salt
1/4 teaspoon ground black pepper
2-3 cups canola oil
2-3 cups marinara sauce — *or vodka sauce*
2 cups shredded mozzarella cheese, divided — *or shredded asiago*
1 cup grated Romano cheese, divided
9 x 13-inch baking pan

INSTRUCTIONS:

Pre-heat the oven to 375 degrees.

PREPARING THE EGGPLANT:

Cut the ends off the eggplants and remove the skin. Lay the eggplant on its side and cut 1/4-inch thick slices, ensuring not to cut slices larger than 1/4 inch.

BREADING THE EGGPLANT:

In a large bowl add the eggs and water and whisk to form an egg wash. In another bowl add 2 cups of breadcrumbs, salt, and pepper and mix well. Dredge each eggplant slice in the egg wash and then the breadcrumbs and place on a baking sheet to stage for cooking. Use the additional cup of breadcrumbs as needed.

EGGPLANT PARMIGIANA...CONTINUED

FRYING THE EGGPLANT:

In a large skillet add 2 cups of canola oil and bring to a high heat. Next, place 3-4 slices of eggplant into hot oil. Once the bottom of the eggplant slice begins to brown (1-2 minutes), flip it and brown the other side (1-2 minutes). Move the eggplant slices to baking sheet and stack between layers of paper towel to strain excess oil. Repeat this process until all eggplant slices have been cooked. Set aside and let the eggplant cool for 10 minutes.

LAYERING THE EGGPLANT:

On the bottom of a 9 x 13-inch baking pan place 1 cup of marinara sauce and spread evenly. Next, cover the bottom of the pan with a layer of eggplant. Spoon about 1/2 cup of marinara sauce evenly over the eggplant. Next, sprinkle 1/2 cup of shredded mozzarella and 1/4 cup of grated cheese on top of the sauce. Repeat this process until the pan is full or until all the eggplant has been used. For the top layer add additional mozzarella and grated cheese if desired.

BAKING THE EGGPLANT:

Cover the pan with aluminum foil and bake for 30 minutes. Remove foil and bake for an additional 10 minutes. Remove from oven and rest for 5 minutes before serving.

TO SERVE:

Serve the eggplant parmigiana with a side of your favorite pasta or a small salad and Italian bread.

APPROXIMATE PREP TIME: 40-50 minutes

APPROXIMATE COOK TIME: 50-60 minutes

EGGPLANT ROLLATINI

SERVES 8

INGREDIENTS:

2 large eggplants *(or 4 zucchini)*
4 large eggs
1/2 cup water
2-3 cups plain breadcrumbs
1/2 teaspoon salt
1/4 teaspoon ground black pepper
2-3 cups canola oil
1-2 pounds ricotta cheese
1 cup shredded mozzarella cheese *(or shredded asiago)*
1 cup grated Romano cheese
1/2 teaspoon garlic powder
2-3 cups marinara sauce, divided *(or vodka sauce)*
9 x 13-inch baking pan

INSTRUCTIONS:

Pre-heat the oven to 375 degrees.

PREPARING THE EGGPLANT:

Begin by cutting the ends off the eggplants and removing the skin. Lay the eggplant on its side and cut 1/4-inch thick slices, ensuring not to cut slices thicker than 1/4 inch.

BREADING THE EGGPLANT:

In a large bowl, add the eggs and water and whisk to form an egg wash. In another bowl add 2 cups of breadcrumbs, salt and ground black pepper and mix well. Dredge each eggplant slice in the egg wash and then the breadcrumbs and place on a baking sheet to stage for cooking. Use the additional cup of breadcrumbs as needed.

EGGPLANT ROLLATINI...CONTINUED

FRYING THE EGGPLANT:

In a large skillet, add 2 cups of canola oil and bring to a high heat. Next, place 3-4 slices of eggplant into hot oil. Once the bottom of the eggplant slice begins to brown (1-2 minutes), flip it and brown the other side (1-2 minutes). Move the eggplant slices to baking sheet and stack between layers of paper towel to strain excess oil. Repeat this process until all eggplant slices have been cooked. Set aside and let the eggplant cool for 10 minutes.

PREPARING THE FILLING:

In a large mixing bowl, combine the ricotta cheese, mozzarella cheese, grated cheese, and garlic powder. Mix well to incorporate all of the ingredients.

ROLLING THE EGGPLANT:

On the bottom of a 9 x 13-inch baking pan, place one cup of marinara sauce and spread evenly. On a flat surface such as a clean cutting board, place an eggplant slice so that you can roll from bottom to top. Using a large tablespoon, place one spoonful of cheese mixture onto the bottom end of the eggplant slice and then roll. Repeat this process until all eggplant slices are filled and rolled. Line the baking pan with the eggplant rolls side-by-side horizontally and spoon the remaining marinara sauce evenly over the top of the eggplant and sprinkle with more grated cheese if desired.

BAKING THE EGGPLANT:

Cover the pan with aluminum foil and bake for 30 minutes. Remove foil and bake for an additional 10 minutes. Remove from oven and rest for 5 minutes before serving.

TO SERVE:

Serve the eggplant rollatini with a side of your favorite pasta or a small salad and Italian bread.

APPROXIMATE PREP TIME:	50-60 minutes
APPROXIMATE COOK TIME:	50-60 minutes

Eggplant Stacks

EGGPLANT STACKS

YIELDS 4-5 STACKS

INGREDIENTS:

1 large eggplant *(or 2 zucchini)*
2 large eggs
1/4 cup water
1 cup plain breadcrumbs
1-2 cups canola oil
1/4 cup extra virgin olive oil
2 tablespoons balsamic vinegar
1 teaspoon salt
1/4 teaspoon ground black pepper
1/2 teaspoon dried oregano
4-6 ounces sun-dried tomatoes *(or 4-6 ounces roasted red peppers)*
8 ounces fresh mozzarella, cut into 8-10 slices *(or sliced asiago or sharp provolone)*
1/4 cup sliced fresh basil

INSTRUCTIONS:

PREPARING THE EGGPLANT:

Begin by cutting the ends off the eggplant and removing all the skin. Next, slice the eggplant in 1/4-inch slices, forming 12-15 flat circles, and set aside. In a large mixing bowl, add the eggs and water and whisk to form an egg wash. In another mixing bowl, add the breadcrumbs. Dredge each eggplant slice in the egg wash and then the breadcrumbs and place on a baking sheet to stage for frying. Repeat this process until all the eggplant is breaded.

EGGPLANT STACKS...CONTINUED

FRYING THE EGGPLANT:

In a large skillet, add 1 cup canola oil and bring to a high heat. Next, place 4-5 slices of eggplant into hot oil, ensuring not to crowd the skillet. Once the bottom of the eggplant slice begins to brown, about 1-2 minutes, flip it over and brown the other side, about 1-2 minutes. Remove finished eggplant slices to baking sheet and stack between layers of paper towels to strain excess oil. Use additional canola oil as needed. Repeat this process until all eggplant slices have been cooked. Set aside and let the eggplant cool for 10 minutes.

PREPARING THE VINAIGRETTE:

In a small bowl, add the extra virgin olive oil, balsamic vinegar, salt, ground black pepper, and dried oregano. Whisk well to incorporate all the ingredients. Set the vinaigrette aside until you are ready to build the eggplant stacks.

STACKING THE EGGPLANT:

To complete one eggplant stack, begin by placing one eggplant slice on a cutting board or flat clean surface. Next, place a slice of fresh mozzarella on top of the eggplant, 2 pieces of sun-dried tomatoes on top of the fresh mozzarella, a pinch of fresh basil on top of the sun-dried tomatoes, and drizzle a small amount of balsamic vinaigrette over the basil (whisk if needed). This will form your first section. Next, repeat this process to form a second complete section. To finish off the complete 2 section eggplant stack, add a final slice of eggplant on top of the second section. Repeat this process until you have 4 complete eggplant stacks.

TO SERVE:

Place the eggplant stacks on a large serving dish and drizzle with more vinaigrette.

APPROXIMATE PREP TIME:	15-25 minutes
APPROXIMATE COOK TIME:	20-30 minutes

CHICKEN

INTRODUCTION TO CHICKEN

This section of the cookbook is filled with my favorite Italian chicken dishes. Growing up, we had chicken a few times a week, so there were plenty of opportunities for me to fall in love with these chicken dishes.

One recipe in this section is very special to me. It was the first meal that I made for my parents: chicken saltimbocca. The first time I made this dish, I was around sixteen years old and decided I wanted to make a fancy meal for my parents. Searching around the house, I found one of my mom's cookbooks. It was one of those that shows you how to prepare everything. It must have been 400 pages, or at least that is how I remember it.

So, there I went, looking through the pages of this book, intimidated by most of the recipes. Then I came across chicken saltimbocca. I remember eating this dish at a wedding one time, and decided I was going to cook it, no matter how difficult it was.

I gathered all the ingredients and went for it. The chicken turned out pretty good, but I overcooked the prosciutto and turned it into jerky. The spinach turned out soggy, but I melted the cheese to perfection. I served the dish to my parents anyway and they were polite and said they enjoyed it.

Over the years, I continued to make this dish and would often serve it when I wanted to impress someone. The recipe is not that difficult, however, it does need some extra time and patience.

A fun recipe to try is the chicken margherita. The combination of fresh, ripe tomatoes and mozzarella is delicious. The fun part of the recipe is when you add the mozzarella at the end. The cheese softens and warms just enough to create a fantastic eating experience.

Have fun cooking these chicken recipes. Pick a few of your favorites, give them a try, and then invent the chicken recipe that works best for you.

Chicken Cacciatore

CHICKEN CACCIATORE

SERVES 4

INGREDIENTS:

1 pound boneless, skinless chicken breasts

1 pound boneless, skinless chicken thighs

1 cup flour

1 teaspoon salt, divided

1/2 teaspoon ground black pepper, divided

1/4 teaspoon onion powder

1/4 teaspoon garlic powder

1/2-1 cup canola oil

1/4 cup extra virgin olive oil

4 garlic cloves, sliced

2 medium sweet onions, sliced

2 green bell peppers, sliced — or 8 ounces roasted red peppers

1 cup of sliced mushrooms — or 1 cup frozen peas

2 medium carrots, sliced — or 4 red bliss potatoes, chopped

1 can (15-16 ounces) diced tomatoes

1/2 cup red wine — or chicken broth

1 cup marinara sauce

INSTRUCTIONS:

PREPARING THE CHICKEN:

Begin by cleaning and trimming the fat from the chicken. Next, cut each chicken breast into 3 even pieces and leave the chicken thighs whole. In a mixing bowl, add the flour, 1/2 teaspoon salt, 1/4 teaspoon ground black pepper, onion powder, and garlic powder and mix well. Next, dredge chicken breast pieces and chicken thighs in the seasoned flour.

CHICKEN CACCIATORE...CONTINUED

COOKING THE CHICKEN:

In a large pot or skillet, add in 1/2 cup canola oil and bring to a high heat. Next, add in the chicken pieces, ensuring not to crowd the skillet, and fry on all sides until golden brown, about 8 minutes total. Remove the chicken from the skillet and set aside. Repeat this process until all the chicken is cooked, then pour off the remaining oil from the skillet. Use more canola oil as needed.

BRINGING EVERYTHING TOGETHER:

In a large pot, add in the extra virgin olive oil and bring to a high heat. Next, add in the garlic and sauté until golden, about 1-2 minutes. Next, add in the onions, bell peppers, mushrooms, carrots, 1/2 teaspoon salt, and 1/4 teaspoon ground black pepper and sauté for 3 minutes on medium heat, mixing occasionally. Next, add in the red wine, diced tomatoes, and marinara sauce. Bring to a simmer and cook for 5 minutes. Finally, add the cooked chicken pieces into the pot and cover. Bring to a simmer and cook for 10 minutes until vegetables are tender, mixing occasionally.

TO SERVE:

Place chicken on a bed of your favorite cooked pasta or serve with a side of roasted potatoes or rice.

APPROXIMATE PREP TIME: 20-30 minutes

APPROXIMATE COOK TIME: 35-45 minutes

CHICKEN FRANCESE

SERVES 4

INGREDIENTS:

4 boneless, skinless chicken breasts (1-2 pounds) *[or boneless pork chops or fillet of flounder]*

1 cup flour

1 teaspoon salt, divided

1/2 teaspoon ground black pepper, divided

1/4 teaspoon onion powder

1/4 teaspoon garlic powder

2 eggs

3/4 cup water, divided

1/2-1 cup canola oil

1/2 stick of unsalted butter

6 garlic cloves, minced

1 cup white wine *[or chicken broth]*

2 cups chicken broth

Juice of 1 lemon

1/4 cup chopped fresh parsley, and more to serve

2 tablespoons cornstarch

6-8 lemon slices, 1/8-inch thick

INSTRUCTIONS:

PREPARING THE CHICKEN:

Begin by cleaning and trimming the fat from the chicken breast. Next, slice the whole chicken breast in half lengthwise to form thinner cutlets. In a mixing bowl, add the flour, 1/2 teaspoon salt, 1/4 teaspoon ground black pepper, onion powder, and garlic powder and mix well. In another mixing bowl, add in the eggs and 1/4 cup water and whisk together to form an egg wash. Next, dredge the cutlets in seasoned flour, then egg wash until all cutlets are coated.

CHICKEN FRANCESE...CONTINUED

COOKING THE CHICKEN:

Place a large skillet on high heat and add in the canola oil. When the oil is hot, add the chicken cutlets to the skillet and fry on both sides until golden brown, about 3-4 minutes each side, ensuring not to crowd the skillet. Remove chicken cutlets from the skillet and set aside. Use more canola oil as needed. Repeat this process until all the chicken is cooked, then pour off the remaining oil from the skillet.

BRINGING EVERYTHING TOGETHER:

In the same large skillet, add in the unsalted butter and melt on medium heat. Next, add the garlic to the unsalted butter and sauté until the garlic begins to turn golden, about 1-2 minutes. Next, add in the white wine, chicken broth, juice of 1 lemon, 1/2 teaspoon salt, 1/4 teaspoon pepper, and fresh parsley. Bring to a simmer and cook for 5 minutes on medium heat. While simmering, in a small bowl, mix the cornstarch and 1/2 cup water together. Next, add the cornstarch mixture to the large skillet and incorporate by stirring for 30 seconds, then simmer the sauce for 5 more minutes on medium heat. Finally, return the chicken to the large skillet and simmer on medium heat for 10 minutes total, turn chicken over after 5 minutes.

TO SERVE:

Place chicken on a bed of your favorite cooked pasta. Add 1 lemon slice to the top of each piece of chicken. Pour or spoon the desired amount of sauce over the chicken. Garnish with fresh parsley.

APPROXIMATE PREP TIME:	20-30 minutes
APPROXIMATE COOK TIME:	30-40 minutes

CHICKEN MARGHERITA

SERVES 4

INGREDIENTS:

4 boneless, skinless chicken breasts (1-2 pounds) — *or boneless pork chops or fillet of fish*

1/2 cup flour

1 teaspoon salt, divided

1/2 teaspoon ground black pepper, divided

1/4 teaspoon onion powder

1/4 teaspoon garlic powder

1/4 cup canola oil

2 tablespoons extra virgin olive oil

4 garlic cloves, thinly sliced

8 ounces of cherry tomatoes, cut in half — *or sun-dried tomatoes*

1/4 cup white wine — *or 1/4 cup water, broth, or balsamic vinegar*

1/2 cup chicken broth

2 tablespoons chopped fresh basil

8 ounces of small fresh mozzarella balls, cut in half — *or 4 ounces asiago cheese or provolone cheese, cubed*

INSTRUCTIONS:

PREPARING THE CHICKEN:

Begin by cleaning and trimming the fat from the chicken breasts. Next, cut the chicken breasts into 1-inch cubes. In a mixing bowl add the flour, 1/2 teaspoon salt, 1/4 teaspoon ground black pepper, onion powder, and garlic powder and mix well. Next, dredge chicken pieces in seasoned flour and set aside.

CHICKEN MARGHERITA...CONTINUED

COOKING THE CHICKEN:

In a large skillet, add in the canola oil and bring to a high heat. Next, add in the chicken pieces, ensuring not to crowd the skillet, and sauté on all sides until golden brown, about 8 minutes total. Remove the chicken from the skillet and set aside. Repeat this process until all the chicken is cooked, then pour off the remaining oil from the skillet.

BRINGING EVERYTHING TOGETHER:

In the same skillet, add in the extra virgin olive oil and bring to a high heat. Next, add in the garlic and sauté until golden, about 1-2 minutes. Next, add in the tomatoes and white wine and cook for 2 minutes on medium heat. Next, add the pre-cooked chicken back into the skillet, chicken broth, 1/2 teaspoon of salt, 1/4 teaspoon of ground black pepper, and fresh basil, and mix well. Bring to a simmer and cook on medium heat for 5 minutes, mixing occasionally. Finally, remove the skillet from the heat, add in the mozzarella balls and mix thoroughly. It is important to remove the skillet from the heat because you do not want to melt the mozzarella, just soften and warm.

TO SERVE:

Serve chicken on a bed of your favorite cooked pasta or serve with a side of roasted potatoes or your favorite whole grain.

APPROXIMATE PREP TIME: 15-20 minutes

APPROXIMATE COOK TIME: 20-30 minutes

CHICKEN MARSALA

SERVES 4

INGREDIENTS:

4 boneless, skinless chicken breasts (1-2 pounds) *(or boneless pork chops or fillet of flounder)*

1 cup flour

1 teaspoon salt, divided

1/2 teaspoon ground black pepper, divided

1/4 teaspoon onion powder

1/4 teaspoon garlic powder

2 eggs

3/4 cup water, divided

1/2 cup canola oil

1/2 stick of unsalted butter

6 garlic cloves, minced

2 cups sliced white button mushrooms *(or 1 can/jar artichoke hearts quartered)*

1 cup Marsala wine

2 cups chicken broth *(or vegetable broth)*

1/4 cup chopped fresh parsley

2 tablespoons cornstarch

INSTRUCTIONS:

PREPARING THE CHICKEN:

Begin by cleaning and trimming the fat from the chicken breasts. Next, slice the whole chicken breasts in half lengthwise to form thinner cutlets. In a mixing bowl add the flour, 1/2 teaspoon salt, 1/4 teaspoon ground black pepper, onion powder, and garlic powder and mix well. In another mixing bowl, add in the eggs and 1/4 cup water and whisk to form an egg wash. Next, dredge the cutlets in the egg wash, then seasoned flour, until all cutlets are coated.

CHICKEN MARSALA...CONTINUED

COOKING THE CHICKEN:

In a large skillet, add in the canola oil and bring to a high heat. Next, add the chicken cutlets to the skillet and fry on both sides until golden brown, about 3-4 minutes each side, ensuring not to crowd the skillet. Remove chicken cutlets from the skillet and set aside. Repeat this process until all of the chicken is cooked, then pour off the remaining oil from the skillet.

BRINGING EVERYTHING TOGETHER:

In the same large skillet, add in the unsalted butter and melt on medium heat. Next, add the minced garlic and sauté until golden, about 1-2 minutes, mixing occasionally. Next, add the mushrooms and cook until they begin to sweat, about 3 minutes. Next, add the Marsala wine, chicken broth, 1/2 teaspoon salt, 1/4 teaspoon ground black pepper, and fresh parsley and mix well. Bring to a simmer then cook for 5 minutes. While simmering, in a small bowl, mix the cornstarch and 1/2 cup water together. Next, add the cornstarch mixture to the skillet and incorporate by stirring for 30 seconds, then simmer the sauce for 5 more minutes on medium heat. Finally, return the chicken to the large skillet and simmer on medium heat for 10 minutes, turning the chicken over once after 5 minutes.

TO SERVE:

Place chicken on a large serving dish. Pour or spoon the desired amount of sauce over the chicken. Garnish with fresh parsley. Best served with roasted potatoes and asparagus.

APPROXIMATE PREP TIME:	20-25 minutes
APPROXIMATE COOK TIME:	35-45 minutes

CHICKEN PARMIGIANA

SERVES 4

INGREDIENTS:

4 boneless, skinless chicken breasts (1-2 pounds) — *or turkey breasts or pork loin*

1 cup plain breadcrumbs — *or flour*

1/2 teaspoon salt

1/4 teaspoon ground black pepper

1/2 teaspoon garlic powder

1/2 teaspoon onion powder

2 eggs

1/4 cup water

1/2 cup canola oil

2-3 cups marinara sauce, divided — *or vodka sauce*

1/2 cup grated Romano cheese

1 cup shredded mozzarella cheese — *or shredded asiago*

INSTRUCTIONS:

Pre-heat the oven to 350 degrees.

PREPARING THE CHICKEN:

Begin by cleaning and trimming the fat from the chicken breasts. Next, slice the whole chicken breasts in half lengthwise to form thinner cutlets. In a mixing bowl add the breadcrumbs, salt, ground black pepper, onion powder, and garlic powder and mix well. In another mixing bowl, add the eggs and water and whisk to form an egg wash. Next, dredge the cutlets in the egg, then breadcrumbs, until all cutlets are coated.

CHICKEN PARMIGIANA...CONTINUED

COOKING THE CHICKEN:

In a large skillet, add in the canola oil and bring to a high heat. Next, add the chicken cutlets to the skillet and fry on both sides until golden brown, about 3-4 minutes each side, ensuring not to crowd the skillet. Remove chicken cutlets from the skillet and set aside. Repeat this process until all the chicken is cooked.

BRINGING EVERYTHING TOGETHER:

On a large baking sheet, add 1 cup of marinara sauce and spread out evenly with a spoon or spatula. Place chicken pieces evenly apart on the baking sheet. With the remaining marinara sauce, spoon the desired amount of sauce over each piece of chicken. Sprinkle grated Romano cheese evenly over the chicken pieces. To finish, sprinkle the shredded mozzarella cheese evenly over the chicken pieces. Bake chicken for 15-20 minutes, until the mozzarella cheese is melted and golden in color.

TO SERVE:

Place chicken on a bed of your favorite cooked pasta (recommend spaghetti or linguini). Enjoy with more marinara sauce, your favorite Italian bread, and a side salad.

APPROXIMATE PREP TIME:	15-20 minutes
APPROXIMATE COOK TIME:	30-40 minutes

CHICKEN PICCATA

SERVES 4

INGREDIENTS:

4 boneless, skinless chicken breasts (1-2 pounds) *(or pork chops or fillet of flounder)*

1 cup flour

1 teaspoon salt, divided

1/2 teaspoon ground black pepper, divided

1/4 teaspoon onion powder

1/4 teaspoon garlic powder

1/2 cup canola oil

1/2 stick of unsalted butter

4 garlic cloves, minced

1 cup white wine

1 cup chicken broth *(or vegetable broth)*

Juice of 1 lemon

1/4 cup chopped fresh parsley

1/4 cup brined capers

2 tablespoons cornstarch

1/2 cup water

INSTRUCTIONS:

PREPARING THE CHICKEN:

Begin by cleaning and trimming the fat from the chicken breasts. Next, slice the whole chicken breasts in half lengthwise to form thinner cutlets. In a mixing bowl, add the flour, 1/2 teaspoon salt, 1/4 teaspoon ground black pepper, onion powder, and garlic powder and mix well. Next, dredge the cutlets in seasoned flour until all cutlets are coated.

CHICKEN PICCATA...CONTINUED

COOKING THE CHICKEN:

In a large skillet, add in the canola oil and bring to a high heat. Next, add the chicken cutlets to the skillet and fry on both sides until golden brown, about 3-4 minutes each side, ensuring not to crowd the skillet. Remove chicken cutlets from the skillet and set aside. Repeat this process until all of the chicken is cooked, then pour off the remaining oil from the skillet.

BRINGING EVERYTHING TOGETHER:

In the same large skillet, add in the unsalted butter and melt on medium heat. Next, add the garlic and sauté until golden, about 1-2 minutes, mixing occasionally. Next, add the white wine, chicken broth, lemon juice, 1/2 teaspoon salt, 1/4 teaspoon ground black pepper, fresh parsley, and capers. Bring to a simmer and cook for 5 minutes. While simmering, in a small bowl, mix the cornstarch and water together. Next, add the cornstarch mixture to the skillet and incorporate by stirring for 30 seconds, then simmer the sauce for 5 more minutes on medium heat. Finally, return the chicken to the large skillet and simmer on medium heat for 10 minutes, turning the chicken over once after 5 minutes.

TO SERVE:

Place chicken on a bed of your favorite cooked pasta (recommend spaghetti or linguini). Pour spoonful of the desired amount of sauce over the chicken. Garnish with fresh parsley.

APPROXIMATE PREP TIME: 20-25 minutes

APPROXIMATE COOK TIME: 35-45 minutes

CHICKEN WITH ROASTED RED PEPPERS

SERVES 4

INGREDIENTS:

4 boneless, skinless chicken breasts (1-2 pounds) *— or pork chops or fillet of flounder*

1/2 cup flour

1 teaspoon salt, divided

1/2 teaspoon ground black pepper, divided

1/2 teaspoon onion powder

1/2 teaspoon garlic powder

1/4 cup canola oil

2 tablespoons extra virgin olive oil

4 garlic cloves, minced

12 ounce jar of roasted red pepper strips *— or artichoke hearts or pitted kalamata olives*

2 tablespoons chopped fresh basil

1/2 cup white wine *— or 1/2 cup broth or 1/4 cup balsamic vinegar*

1 tablespoons cornstarch

1/4 cup water

1/2 cup chicken broth *— or vegetable broth*

INSTRUCTIONS:

PREPARING THE CHICKEN:

Begin by cleaning and trimming the fat from the chicken breasts. Next, cut the chicken breasts into 1-inch cubes. In a mixing bowl add the flour, 1/2 teaspoon salt, 1/4 teaspoon ground black pepper, onion powder, and garlic powder and mix well. Next, dredge chicken pieces in seasoned flour and set aside.

CHICKEN WITH ROASTED RED PEPPERS...CONTINUED

COOKING THE CHICKEN:

In a large skillet, add the canola oil and bring to a high heat. Next, add in the chicken pieces, ensuring not to crowd the skillet, and fry on all sides until golden brown, about 6 minutes total. Remove the chicken from the skillet and set aside. Repeat this process until all the chicken is cooked, then pour off the remaining oil from the skillet.

BRINGING EVERYTHING TOGETHER:

In the same skillet add the extra virgin olive oil and bring to a high heat. Next, add in the garlic and sauté until golden, about 1-2 minutes. Next, add in the roasted red peppers and white wine and cook for 2 minutes on medium heat. Next, add the pre-cooked chicken back into the skillet, chicken broth, 1/4 teaspoon of salt, 1/4 teaspoon of ground black pepper, and fresh basil, and mix well. Bring to a simmer and cook on medium heat for 5 minutes, mixing occasionally. While simmering, in a small bowl, mix the cornstarch and water together. Next, add the cornstarch mixture to the skillet and incorporate by stirring for 30 seconds, then simmer the sauce for 5 more minutes on medium heat.

TO SERVE:

Place chicken in a large serving dish. Alternatively, serve chicken on a bed of your favorite cooked pasta, or serve with a side of roasted potatoes or rice.

APPROXIMATE PREP TIME: 15-20 minutes

APPROXIMATE COOK TIME: 20-30 minutes

Chicken Saltimbocca

CHICKEN SALTIMBOCCA

SERVES 4

INGREDIENTS:

4 boneless, skinless chicken breasts (1-2 pounds) — *or turkey breasts or boneless pork chops*

1/2 cup flour

1/2 teaspoon salt

1/2 teaspoon ground black pepper

1/2 teaspoon garlic powder

1/2 teaspoon onion powder

1/4 cup canola oil

1 cup chicken stock

16 ounces fresh baby spinach — *or Swiss chard*

2 tablespoons extra virgin olive oil

2 garlic cloves, sliced

8 thin slices of prosciutto — *or 8 slices bacon, pancetta, or ham*

8 slices of fontina cheese — *or 8 slices Swiss, asiago, or mozzarella cheese*

INSTRUCTIONS:

Pre-heat the oven to 350 degrees.

PREPARING THE CHICKEN:

Begin by cleaning and trimming the fat from the chicken breasts. Next, slice the whole chicken breasts in half lengthwise to form thinner cutlets. In a mixing bowl, add the flour, salt, ground black pepper, onion powder, and garlic powder and mix well. Next, dredge the cutlets in seasoned flour until all cutlets are coated.

CHICKEN SALTIMBOCCA...CONTINUED

COOKING THE CHICKEN:

In a large skillet, add the canola oil and bring to a high heat. Next, add in the chicken cutlets, ensuring not to crowd the skillet, and fry on both sides until golden brown, about 2-3 minutes per side. Remove chicken cutlets from the skillet and set aside. Repeat this process until all the chicken is cooked, then pour off the remaining oil from the skillet. Return the skillet to high heat, add 1 cup of chicken broth, and bring to a simmer. Lower to medium heat and return chicken to the pan. Simmer chicken on medium heat for 5 minutes, flipping once. Remove the chicken and place on a baking pan, pour the remaining liquid over the chicken.

COOKING THE SPINACH:

Return the skillet to high heat and add 2 tablespoons of extra virgin olive oil. Next, add the garlic and sauté until golden, about 1-2 minutes. Turn heat to low and add half of the spinach, stirring occasionally until the spinach is reduced by half, about 1 minute. Next, add the remaining spinach and mix well to combine with the garlic. Cook until the spinach is reduced by half again, about 1 minute, then remove from the heat.

BRINGING EVERYTHING TOGETHER:

Spoon enough spinach to cover a chicken cutlet, then place one slice of prosciutto on top of the spinach, and one slice of fontina cheese on top of the prosciutto. Repeat this step until all the chicken has spinach, prosciutto, and fontina cheese on top. Place any remaining spinach around the chicken fillets on the baking sheet and bake at 350 degrees until the cheese melts, about 10-15 minutes.

TO SERVE:

Place the chicken in the center of a large serving dish and place the spinach next to the chicken.

APPROXIMATE PREP TIME:	15-20 minutes
APPROXIMATE COOK TIME:	35-45 minutes

CHICKEN VODKA WITH BROCCOLI

SERVES 4

INGREDIENTS:

4 boneless, skinless chicken breasts (1-2 pounds) *— or boneless pork loin*

1/2 cup flour

1 teaspoon salt, divided

1/2 teaspoon ground black pepper, divided

1/2 teaspoon garlic powder

1/2 teaspoon onion powder

1/4 cup canola oil

2 tablespoons extra virgin olive oil

4 garlic cloves, sliced

4 cups of broccoli florets *— or asparagus, green beans, or cauliflower*

16-24 ounces vodka sauce *— or marinara sauce*

INSTRUCTIONS:

PREPARING THE CHICKEN:

Begin by cleaning and trimming the fat from the chicken breasts. Next, cut the whole chicken breast into 1-inch cubes. In a mixing bowl add the flour, 1/2 teaspoon salt, 1/4 teaspoon ground black pepper, garlic powder, and onion powder and mix well. Next, dredge the chicken in seasoned flour until all pieces are coated.

COOKING THE CHICKEN:

In a large pot or skillet, add in the canola oil and bring to a high heat. Next, add in the chicken pieces, ensuring not to crowd the skillet, and fry on all sides until golden brown, about 6 minutes total. Remove the chicken from the skillet and set aside. Repeat this process until all of the chicken is cooked, then pour off the remaining oil from the skillet.

CHICKEN VODKA WITH BROCCOLI...CONTINUED

BRINGING EVERYTHING TOGETHER:

In the same skillet, add in the extra virgin olive oil and bring to a high heat. Next, add in the garlic and sauté until golden, about 1-2 minutes. Next, add in the broccoli florets, 1/2 teaspoon of salt, and 1/4 teaspoon of ground black pepper and sauté for 5 minutes, mixing occasionally. Next add the chicken back into the skillet and 4 cups of vodka sauce. Bring to a simmer and then cook for 5 minutes, mixing occasionally.

TO SERVE:

Place chicken vodka with broccoli on a bed of your favorite cooked pasta.

APPROXIMATE PREP TIME:	15-20 minutes
APPROXIMATE COOK TIME:	30-40 minutes

CHICKEN WITH ZUCCHINI AND BEANS

SERVES 4

INGREDIENTS:

1/4 cup canola oil

4 boneless, skinless chicken breasts (1-2 pounds), cut into bite-size pieces — *or boneless pork loin or turkey breasts*

4 garlic cloves, sliced

2 medium zucchini, cut into 1/2-inch by 3-inch sticks

1 can (15-16 ounces) cannellini beans (with liquid) — *or great northern or navy beans*

1 teaspoon salt

1/2 teaspoon ground black pepper

1 can (15-16 ounces) diced tomatoes — *or 4 plum tomatoes, diced*

INSTRUCTIONS:

PREPARING THE CHICKEN:

In a large skillet, add in the canola oil and bring to a high heat. Next, add in the chicken and sauté until golden brown on all sides, about 4-6 minutes total, mixing occasionally. Remove the chicken from the skillet and set aside.

PREPARING THE VEGETABLES:

Return the skillet to medium heat, add in the garlic and sauté until golden, about 1-2 minutes. Next, add in the zucchini and sauté for 4 minutes, mixing occasionally. Next, add in the beans, tomatoes, salt, and ground black pepper. Bring to a simmer and cook for 2 minutes, mixing occasionally. Finally, add the cooked chicken back into the skillet, bring to a simmer, and cook for 5 minutes, mixing occasionally.

TO SERVE:

Place the chicken with zucchini on top of a bed of your favorite pasta or whole grain.

APPROXIMATE PREP TIME: 20-25 minutes
APPROXIMATE COOK TIME: 25-35 minutes

STUFFED CHICKEN BREASTS

SERVES 4

INGREDIENTS:

4 boneless, skinless chicken breasts (1-2 pounds) *(or boneless pork loin or turkey breasts)*

2 tablespoons extra virgin olive oil

5 garlic cloves, sliced

1 large onion, sliced

5 white button mushrooms, sliced

5 plum tomatoes, chopped *(or 1 can (15-16 ounces) diced tomatoes)*

1/2 cup white wine

1 teaspoon salt, divided

1/2 teaspoon ground black pepper, divided

12 ounces baby spinach *(or 12 ounces Swiss chard or kale)*

Butcher's twine or toothpicks

1/2 teaspoon paprika

INSTRUCTIONS:

Pre-heat the oven to 375 degrees.

PREPARING THE CHICKEN:

Butterfly (slice the chicken breast lengthwise 3/4 of the way through) the chicken breasts and set aside.

PREPARING THE STUFFING:

In a large skillet, add in the extra virgin olive oil and bring to a high heat. Next, add in the garlic and sauté until golden, about 1-2 minutes. Next, add the onion, mushrooms, tomatoes, white wine, 1/2 teaspoon salt, and 1/4 teaspoon pepper and bring to a simmer. Cook for 5 minutes, mixing occasionally. Finally, add the fresh spinach and cook until soft, about 1-2 minutes, mixing occasionally. Remove from the heat and set aside.

STUFFED CHICKEN BREASTS...CONTINUED

STUFFING THE CHICKEN:

On a large cutting board, lay out butterflied chicken breast. Add enough stuffing to cover one side of the chicken breast, about 2 tablespoons, and then fold over the remaining half of the chicken breast. Next, using the butcher's twine, tie the chicken together to hold in the stuffing and then place on a baking sheet. Repeat this process until all the chicken is stuffed, tied, and placed on the baking sheet.

COOKING THE CHICKEN:

Season the top of the chicken with 1/2 teaspoon salt, 1/4 teaspoon ground black pepper, and 1/2 teaspoon paprika. Place the chicken into the oven and bake at 375 degrees for 40 minutes, or until the internal temperature of the chicken is 160 degrees.

TO SERVE:

Serve with a side of roasted potatoes or your favorite whole grain.

APPROXIMATE PREP TIME:	30-40 minutes
APPROXIMATE COOK TIME:	50-60 minutes

RED MEAT

INTRODUCTION TO RED MEAT

This section of the cookbook is all my favorite Italian meat dishes. This includes beef, pork, and veal. Growing up, my mom made the American staple home-cooked meals. This included meatballs, meatloaf, and beef stew. But she put an Italian twist to them by making the dishes with marinara sauce instead of the traditional brown gravy. I came to love these recipes with the marinara sauce. I have continued to make them this way and shared them here in this cookbook.

I am particularly fond of the beef stew recipe. I can remember many fall and winter weekend days waking up to the smell of marinara sauce and beef stew, and particularly the smell of garlic and onions. The cool crisp air and the excitement of a full day of watching football was the appetizer. The delicious beef stew was the main event. I have many fond memories from those days.

My mom would prepare the stew before football started. This way the entire family could watch the games together. Then, around 5:00 p.m., the stew was heated, the Italian bread was toasted, and then the eating would begin.

There is something unique about the way I eat my beef stew that I want to share. To this day, it is still somewhat of a conversation topic when I sit down with my parents to eat this dish. As a little kid, my mom would mash up the potatoes and carrots in the stew. This way I would eat the vegetables without knowing what they were. The effect of this was amazing to me. It created a delicious, mashed vegetable stew, which I absolutely love. Well into adulthood, I continue to eat my beef stew this way! I mash up my own vegetables now.

Over the years, I have experimented with the ingredients in the beef stew. However, I tend to gravitate back to a variation of the beef stew that my mom prepared so many times for us. The beef stew recipe in this book is an homage to that time in my life and the many great memories from those days.

Another one of my favorite meat recipes is sausage with broccoli rabe. The combination of the sweet Italian sausage and the slight bitterness of the broccoli rabe is delicious. I make my own Italian sausage which allows me to control the fat content, cut of meat used, and added ingredients. I haven't written up the recipe or process yet. I do intend to write it up someday, either for another cookbook, or for a feature post on the blog.

BEEF AND BROCCOLI

SERVES 4

INGREDIENTS:

2 tablespoons canola oil

2 pounds beef London broil sliced into thin, bite-size strips *(or pork cubes or chicken cubes)*

1 teaspoon salt, divided

1/2 teaspoon ground black pepper, divided

1/4 cup extra virgin olive oil

4 garlic cloves, minced

8 cups fresh broccoli florets (2-3 large heads of broccoli)

1/2 cup red wine

1 cup beef broth *(or chicken or vegetable broth)*

1/4 cup of Worcestershire sauce

2 tablespoons cornstarch

1/4 cup water

INSTRUCTIONS:

PREPARING THE BEEF:

In a large skillet, add in the canola oil and bring to a high heat. Next, add beef slices, 1/2 teaspoon of salt, and 1/4 teaspoon ground black pepper, ensuring not to crowd the skillet. Sauté until beef is rare, about 3-4 minutes, stirring occasionally. Remove beef from skillet, set aside, and pour off the remaining oil.

BEEF AND BROCCOLI...CONTINUED

BRINGING EVERYTHING TOGETHER:

Place skillet back on high heat and add in the extra virgin olive oil. Next, add the garlic and sauté until golden, about 1-2 minutes. Next, add the broccoli florets and sauté for 5 minutes, mixing occasionally. Next add the pre-cooked beef back into the skillet, red wine, beef broth, 1/2 teaspoon of salt, 1/4 teaspoon ground black pepper, and Worcestershire sauce. Bring to a simmer and cook for 5 minutes. Next, in a small bowl, whisk the cornstarch and water together. Finally, add the cornstarch mixture to the large skillet, bring to a simmer, and cook for 5 minutes, mixing occasionally.

TO SERVE:

Serve with a side of roasted potatoes or your favorite whole grain.

APPROXIMATE PREP TIME: 15-20 minutes

APPROXIMATE COOK TIME: 25-30 minutes

Beef Stew Italian Style

BEEF STEW ITALIAN STYLE

SERVES 4

INGREDIENTS:

2 pounds beef stew meat *(or turkey, chicken, or pork cut into cubes)*

2 tablespoons extra virgin olive oil

1/2 teaspoon salt

1/4 teaspoon ground black pepper

5 garlic cloves, sliced

1 large onion, sliced

5 medium white button mushrooms, sliced *(or 1 cup peas, 4 ounces sun-dried tomatoes)*

4 red bliss potatoes, cut into bite-size pieces *(or fingerling or yellow potatoes)*

4 carrots, cut into bite-size pieces

24 ounces marinara sauce

INSTRUCTIONS:

PREPARING THE STEW:

In a large pot, add the extra virgin olive oil and bring to a high heat. Next, add in the stew meat, salt, and ground black pepper and sauté for 2 minutes, mixing occasionally. Next, add in the garlic and onion and sauté for 2 minutes, mixing occasionally. Next, add the mushrooms, potatoes, and carrots and sauté for 2 minutes, mixing occasionally. Finally, add in the marinara sauce and bring to a simmer. Lower to a medium-low heat and simmer for 30 minutes, or until potatoes and carrots are tender, mixing occasionally.

TO SERVE:

Place the stew in a large bowl and serve family-style with crusty Italian bread.

APPROXIMATE PREP TIME: 20-25 minutes

APPROXIMATE COOK TIME: 40-50 minutes

MEATBALLS

YIELDS 18-24

INGREDIENTS:

2 pounds ground beef (80/20) *(or ground turkey, chicken, or pork)*

3 eggs

1 cup plain breadcrumbs

1/4 cup grated Romano cheese *(or Parmigiano Reggiano or asiago)*

1/2 teaspoon salt

1/4 teaspoon ground black pepper

1/2 teaspoon garlic powder

1/2 teaspoon onion powder

1/2 teaspoon dried oregano

INSTRUCTIONS:

PREPARING THE MEATBALLS:

Add all ingredients into a large bowl and mix together well. Ensure all ingredients are mixed thoroughly and evenly. Once mixture is prepared you are ready to form the meatballs. Spoon out the desired amount of mixture (1 heaping tablespoon is recommended) and roll in between your hands until a uniform ball is formed. Continue this until the entire mixture is used.

COOKING THE MEATBALLS:

Place a large skillet on medium heat and add the meatballs, ensuring not to crowd the skillet. Cook until all sides are browned, about 2-3 minutes per side (about 12 minutes total). Rotate meatballs on all sides to ensure the mixture is cooked throughout. Repeat this process until all the meatballs are cooked.

MEATBALLS...CONTINUED

ALTERNATIVE COOKING METHOD 1:

Place formed meatballs on a baking sheet and cook for 30-35 minutes at 375 degrees or until the meatballs reach an internal temperature of 160 degrees.

ALTERNATIVE COOKING METHOD 2:

Bring 24 ounces marinara sauce to a simmer and add in the uncooked meatballs. Cook for 30 minutes on simmer. Stir occasionally to ensure even distribution of heat.

TO SERVE:

Serve with spaghetti or your favorite pasta.

APPROXIMATE PREP TIME: 15-25 minutes
APPROXIMATE COOK TIME: 15-25 minutes

MEATLOAF ITALIAN STYLE

SERVES 4

INGREDIENTS:

2 pounds ground beef (80/20) — *or ground turkey, chicken, or pork*

16 ounces marinara sauce, plus more to serve

3 eggs

1 cup plain breadcrumbs

1/4 cup grated Romano cheese — *or Parmigiano Reggiano or asiago*

1/2 teaspoon salt

1/4 teaspoon ground black pepper

1/2 teaspoon garlic powder

1/2 teaspoon onion powder

1/2 teaspoon dried oregano

INSTRUCTIONS:

Pre-heat the oven to 375 degrees.

PREPARING THE MEATLOAF:

Add all ingredients in a large bowl and mix well together. Ensure all ingredients are mixed thoroughly and evenly. Once mixture is prepared, you are ready to form the meatloaf. With your hands, form the meatloaf mix into the shape of a loaf and place on a baking sheet or pan. Next, spoon the marinara sauce evenly over the meatloaf. Finally, bake for 30-35 minutes, or until the internal temperature of the meatloaf is 160 degrees.

TO SERVE:

Cut the meatloaf into 1-inch-thick slices and place on a serving dish with a side of marinara sauce. Pair with pasta or roasted potatoes.

APPROXIMATE PREP TIME: 10-15 minutes

APPROXIMATE COOK TIME: 30-35 minutes

Pork with Beans and Tomatoes

PORK WITH BEANS AND TOMATOES

SERVES 4

INGREDIENTS:

4 boneless pork chops

1/4 cup canola oil

4 garlic cloves, sliced

1 can (15-16 ounces) diced tomatoes *or 4 plum tomatoes, diced or 6 ounces sun-dried tomatoes, sliced*

1 can (15-16 ounces) navy beans (with liquid) *or cannellini, kidney, or pinto beans*

1/2 teaspoon salt

1/4 teaspoon ground black pepper

INSTRUCTIONS:

PREPARING THE PORK:

Begin by cutting the boneless pork chops into 1-inch cubes. In a large skillet, add in the canola oil and bring to a high heat. Next, add in the garlic and sauté until golden, about 1-2 minutes. Lower to medium heat, add in the pork, salt, and ground black pepper and sauté on all sides until golden brown, about 5-7 minutes total, mixing occasionally.

BRINGING EVERYTHING TOGETHER:

Continuing on medium heat, add in the tomatoes and beans and bring to a simmer. Finally, cook for 10 minutes, mixing occasionally.

TO SERVE:

Serve the pork with beans and tomatoes on a bed of pasta or your favorite whole grain.

APPROXIMATE PREP TIME: 5-10 minutes

APPROXIMATE COOK TIME: 20-25 minutes

SAUSAGE AND BROCCOLI RABE

SERVES 4

INGREDIENTS:

2 bunches broccoli rabe

6 sweet Italian sausage links *(or chicken sausage or turkey sausage)*

1/2 cup extra virgin olive oil

5 garlic cloves, thinly sliced

1 cup chicken broth *(or vegetable broth)*

1/2 teaspoon salt

1/4 teaspoon ground black pepper

Crushed red pepper to taste

INSTRUCTIONS:

PREPARING THE SAUSAGE WITH BROCCOLI RABE:

Begin by removing the bottom third portion of each broccoli rabe stem and set aside. Next, cut the sausage into 1/2-inch slices. In a large pot, add in the sliced sausage and sauté on all sides on high heat until the sausage begins to brown, about 3 minutes. Next, add in the extra virgin olive oil and garlic and sauté until the garlic begins to turn golden, about 1-2 minutes. Reduce to medium heat and add in broccoli rabe, salt, and ground black pepper and sauté for 5 minutes, mixing occasionally. Next, add in the chicken broth and crushed red pepper flakes. Simmer for 5 minutes or until broccoli rabe is tender, mixing occasionally to incorporate all ingredients.

TO SERVE:

Serve on a bed of your favorite pasta or with a side of roasted potatoes.

APPROXIMATE PREP TIME: 10-15 minutes

APPROXIMATE COOK TIME: 15-25 minutes

SAUSAGE WITH PEPPERS AND ONIONS

SERVES 4

INGREDIENTS:

6 sweet Italian sausage links *(or chicken sausage or turkey sausage)*

4 garlic cloves, sliced

2 red bell peppers, sliced

2 yellow bell peppers, sliced

2 large, sweet onions, sliced

1/2 teaspoon salt

1/4 teaspoon ground black pepper

16 ounces of marinara sauce *(or 2 cans (15-16 ounces) diced tomatoes (with liquid))*

INSTRUCTIONS:

PREPARING THE SAUSAGE:

Bring a large skillet to medium heat. Add in the sausage links and cook for 8 minutes, flipping the sausage a few times. Remove from skillet, cut the sausage into 1/2-inch slices, and set aside.

PREPARING THE PEPPERS AND ONIONS:

Place the same skillet on high heat and add in the garlic. Sauté until the garlic begins to turn golden, about 1-2 minutes. Next add the red and yellow bell peppers, sweet onions, salt, and ground black pepper. Sauté for 5-7 minutes until peppers and onions are tender, mixing occasionally.

BRINGING EVERYTHING TOGETHER:

Add the sausage and marinara sauce into the skillet with the vegetables and bring to a simmer. Cook for 10 minutes, mixing occasionally.

TO SERVE:

Place sausage, peppers, and onions into a large serving bowl. Alternatively, serve as a sandwich on Italian bread or long Italian rolls.

APPROXIMATE PREP TIME: 15-20 minutes

APPROXIMATE COOK TIME: 20-30 minutes

STEAK PIZZAIOLA

SERVES 4

INGREDIENTS:

2 tablespoons extra virgin olive oil

4 garlic cloves, minced

2 pounds beef London broil, sliced into thin bite-size strips *(or boneless chicken breasts or boneless pork loin cut into stripes)*

1/2 cup red wine

1/2 teaspoon salt

1/4 teaspoon ground black pepper

2 bell peppers, sliced

2 sweet onions, sliced

1 cup marinara sauce *(or 1 can (15-16 ounces) diced tomatoes)*

INSTRUCTIONS:

PREPARING THE STEAK PIZZAIOLA:

In a large pot or skillet, add in the extra virgin olive oil and bring to a high heat. Next, add in the garlic and sauté until golden, about 1-2 minutes. Next, add in the beef, red wine, salt, and ground black pepper. Bring to a simmer and cook for 3 minutes, mixing occasionally. Next, add in the bell peppers and sweet onions and sauté for 5 minutes, mixing occasionally. Finally, add in the marinara sauce and bring to a simmer. Cook for 10 minutes, mixing occasionally.

TO SERVE:

Place in a large serving dish and serve as a stand-alone dish or with a side of your favorite pasta.

APPROXIMATE PREP TIME: 15-20 minutes

APPROXIMATE COOK TIME: 20-25 minutes

VEAL CUTLETS

SERVES 4

INGREDIENTS:

1 cup plain breadcrumbs *(or flour)*

1 teaspoon salt

1/2 teaspoon ground black pepper

1/2 teaspoon garlic powder

1/2 teaspoon onion powder

2 eggs

1/4 cup water

1/4 cup grated Romano cheese *(or grated Parmigiano Reggiano or asiago)*

1 cup canola oil

8 thinly sliced veal cutlets *(or 4 boneless chicken breasts or 4 boneless pork chops)*

INSTRUCTIONS:

PREPARING THE VEAL:

In a large mixing bowl, combine the breadcrumbs, salt, ground black pepper, garlic powder, and onion powder, and mix well. In a medium mixing bowl add the eggs, water, and Romano cheese and whisk to form an egg wash. For each veal cutlet, dredge in egg then breadcrumbs, and set aside. Repeat until all the veal cutlets are coated.

COOKING THE VEAL:

In a large skillet, add the canola oil and bring to a high heat. Next, add in the veal cutlets, ensuring not to crowd the skillet, and fry on both sides until golden brown, about 2 minutes a side. Remove the veal from the skillet and set aside. Repeat this process until all the veal is cooked.

TO SERVE:

Serve veal with a side of roasted potatoes or rice. Alternatively, place the veal cutlet on crusty Italian bread with your favorite dipping sauce.

APPROXIMATE PREP TIME: 10-15 minutes

APPROXIMATE COOK TIME: 10-15 minutes

VEAL WITH PROSCIUTTO

SERVES 4

INGREDIENTS:

1/2 cup flour

1/2 teaspoon salt

1/2 teaspoon garlic powder

1/2 teaspoon onion powder

1/4 teaspoon ground black pepper

2 tablespoons extra virgin olive oil

8 thinly sliced veal cutlets *or 4 boneless chicken breasts or 4 boneless pork chops*

3 garlic cloves, minced

3 shallots, minced

1/2 cup white wine

Grated Romano cheese to taste

1/2 pound sliced prosciutto *or pancetta or bacon*

INSTRUCTIONS:

PREPARING THE VEAL:

In a mixing bowl add the flour, salt, ground black pepper, onion powder, and garlic powder and mix well. Next, dredge the cutlets in seasoned flour until all cutlets are coated.

COOKING THE VEAL:

Place a large skillet on high heat and add in the extra virgin olive oil. When the oil is hot, add the veal cutlets to the skillet and fry on both sides until golden brown, about 1 minute each side, ensuring not to crowd the skillet. Remove veal cutlets from the skillet and set aside. Repeat this process until all the veal is cooked.

VEAL WITH PROSCIUTTO...CONTINUED

BRINGING EVERYTHING TOGETHER:

Return the skillet to high heat and add in the garlic and sauté until golden, about 1-2 minutes. Next, add in the prosciutto and shallots and sauté for 2 minutes, mixing occasionally. Next, return the veal to the skillet, add in the wine, and bring to a simmer. Cook for 4 minutes, flipping the veal one time.

TO SERVE:

Arrange veal on dinner plates with prosciutto on top of each piece. Drizzle liquid from the pan over veal and sprinkle with parmesan cheese. Serve with a side of vegetables and roasted potatoes or your favorite whole grain.

APPROXIMATE PREP TIME:	15-20 minutes
APPROXIMATE COOK TIME:	20-25 minutes

VEAL AND PEPPERS

SERVES 4

INGREDIENTS:

2 tablespoons extra virgin olive oil

4 garlic cloves, minced

3 bell peppers, sliced

1/2 teaspoon salt

8 veal cutlets cut into strips *(or 4 boneless chicken breasts or 4 boneless pork chops)*

1/4 teaspoon ground black pepper

1/2 cup red wine

2 cups marinara sauce *(or 2 cans of diced tomatoes (15-16 ounce cans))*

1/2 teaspoon dried oregano

INSTRUCTIONS:

PREPARING THE VEAL AND PEPPERS:

In a large skillet, add the extra virgin olive oil and bring to a high heat. Next, add in the garlic and sauté until golden, about 1-2 minutes. Next, add in the peppers, salt, and ground black pepper, and sauté for 2 minutes, mixing occasionally. Next, add in the veal strips and sauté for 2 minutes, mixing occasionally. Finally, add in the red wine, marinara sauce, and oregano and bring to a simmer. Cook for 10 minutes, mixing occasionally, until the peppers are tender and the sauce thickens.

TO SERVE:

Place in a large serving dish and serve as a stand-alone dish or with a side of your favorite pasta or roasted potatoes.

APPROXIMATE PREP TIME: 10-15 minutes

APPROXIMATE COOK TIME: 15-20 minutes

SEAFOOD

INTRODUCTION TO SEAFOOD

In this cookbook, I offer a few staple seafood recipes that have their origin from my childhood. I must admit that seafood is my least favorite food to eat. I have tried many types of seafood and fish; I don't care for it like I do other food.

Most of these dishes come together quickly. One exception is the fried baccalà recipe, which requires preparing the fish overnight. That recipe calls for dried cod. The dried cod is salt preserved and requires soaking and rinsing the fish for 24 hours in fresh cold water. After changing the water a few times over the course of a day, the cod is ready for frying.

The fried calamari recipe is one that I prepare every Christmas Eve. My entire family looks forward to the fried calamari and it brings me joy to cook that dish for everyone. I have found that my favorite way to cook the calamari dish is with a bit of seasoned flour on the squid. With this method, the squid fries up perfectly with a light crispy coating. It is amazing with some homemade marinara sauce!

Another one of my favorite seafood recipes is shrimp scampi. It is quite easy to make. The recipe comes together in one skillet and the flavors are outstanding.

Have fun cooking these seafood recipes. Pick a few of your favorites, give them a try, and then invent the seafood recipe that works the best for you.

ANCHOVY PASTA

SERVES 4

INGREDIENTS:

1 pound uncooked spaghetti *(or your favorite pasta)*

1/2 cup starchy water from cooking the spaghetti

4 anchovy fillets in oil, chopped

1/4 cup extra virgin olive oil

4 garlic cloves, sliced

1/2 teaspoon salt

1/4 teaspoon crushed red pepper

1/2 cup grated Parmigiano Reggiano cheese *(or finely shredded asiago)*

INSTRUCTIONS:

PREPARING THE PASTA:

Prepare the spaghetti according to the package instructions for al dente pasta. Before straining the spaghetti, remove 1/2 cup of starchy water and set aside.

BRINGING EVERYTHING TOGETHER:

While spaghetti is cooking, in a large skillet add the extra virgin olive oil and bring to a high heat. Next, add in the anchovies and sauté for 1 minute, mixing occasionally. Next, add in the garlic, salt, and crushed red pepper and sauté for 2 minutes, mixing occasionally. Finally, add in the cooked spaghetti, grated Parmigiano Reggiano cheese, and starchy water and cook for 3 minutes, mixing occasionally.

TO SERVE:

Place pasta in a large serving bowl. Add more parmesan cheese to taste.

APPROXIMATE PREP TIME: 10-15 minutes

APPROXIMATE COOK TIME: 15-20 minutes

CALAMARI MARINARA

SERVES 4

INGREDIENTS:

1 pound linguini *(or spaghetti or angel hair)*

2 tablespoons extra virgin olive oil

4 garlic cloves, sliced

16 ounces squid, cleaned *(or 16 ounces shrimp or 16 ounces scallops)*

1 teaspoon salt

1/2 teaspoon ground black pepper

24 ounces marinara sauce

1/4 cup fresh basil, rough chopped

INSTRUCTIONS:

PREPARING THE PASTA:

Prepare the pasta according to the package instructions for al dente pasta. Strain pasta and set aside.

PREPARING THE CALAMARI:

While the pasta is cooking, begin by separating the calamari bodies from the tentacles. Leave the tentacles whole. Next, cut the calamari bodies into 1/2-inch rings. Set aside the calamari pieces.

COOKING THE CALAMARI:

In a large pot, add the extra virgin olive oil and bring to a high heat. Next, add in the garlic and sauté until golden, about 1-2 minutes. Next, add in the squid, salt, and pepper and sauté for 2 minutes, mixing occasionally. Finally, add in the marinara sauce and basil and bring to a simmer. Cook for 10 minutes, mixing occasionally.

BRINGING EVERYTHING TOGETHER:

To the pot, add in the cooked spaghetti and cook for 2 minutes, mixing occasionally, or until the spaghetti is hot.

TO SERVE:

Place the calamari marinara in a large serving bowl and serve with toasted Italian bread.

APPROXIMATE PREP TIME: 15-20 minutes

APPROXIMATE COOK TIME: 20-30 minutes

FRIED BACCALA

SERVES 4

INGREDIENTS:

- 1 pound dried, salted cod fish *(or 16 ounces shrimp or 16 ounces scallops)*
- 1 cup all-purpose flour *(or plain breadcrumbs)*
- 1 teaspoon salt
- 1 teaspoon ground black pepper
- 1 egg
- 1 cup of canola oil for frying

INSTRUCTIONS:

RINSING THE COD:

To remove the salt from the dried cod, you will need to soak the cod in cold water for 24 hours. In a large mixing bowl, place the dried cod in fresh water and cover. Place the cod into the refrigerator and let soak for a few hours. Repeat this process 3-4 more times over the course of 24 hours. Finally, remove the cod from the water, rinse, and lay out on paper towels.

PREPARING THE COD:

In a mixing bowl, add the flour, salt, ground black pepper and mix well. In another mixing bowl, add in the egg and whisk to form an egg wash. Next, dredge the cod in the egg and then the seasoned flour until all pieces are coated.

COOKING THE COD:

In a large skillet, add the canola oil and bring to a high heat. Next, add in the cod pieces, ensuring not to crowd the skillet, and fry on both sides until golden brown, about 4 minutes total.

TO SERVE:

Place the fried baccalà on a serving dish. Garnish with lemon wedges, kalamata olives, and fresh parsley or serve with your favorite dipping sauce.

APPROXIMATE PREP TIME: 24 hours

APPROXIMATE COOK TIME: 10-15 minutes

Fried Calamari

FRIED CALAMARI

SERVES 4

INGREDIENTS:

- 1 cup all-purpose flour *(or plain breadcrumbs)*
- 1 teaspoon salt
- 1 teaspoon ground black pepper
- 16 ounces squid, cleaned *(or 16 ounces shrimp or 16 ounces scallops)*
- 3 cups of canola oil
- 1/4 cup chopped fresh parsley
- 4 lemon wedges

INSTRUCTIONS:

PREPARING THE CALAMARI:

Begin by rinsing the squid with cold water. Next, separate the squid bodies from the tentacles. Cut the bodies into 1/2-inch rings and leave the tentacles whole. In a large mixing bowl, combine flour, salt, and ground black pepper and mix well. In small batches, add the squid to the flour mixture and coat thoroughly, ensuring to shake off excess flour. Set the coated squid aside.

COOKING THE CALAMARI:

In a large pot, add the canola oil and bring to a high heat. When the oil is hot, place the coated squid into the oil in small batches. Fry for 5-7 minutes until the squid is golden in color, mixing occasionally to ensure the squid does not stick together. Remove squid from oil and strain on paper towels. Repeat the process until all the squid is cooked.

TO SERVE:

Place fried calamari on a serving dish and garnish with lemon wedges and fresh parsley. Serve with a side of marinara or your favorite dipping sauce.

APPROXIMATE PREP TIME: 10-15 minutes

APPROXIMATE COOK TIME: 20-30 minutes

MUSSELS AND WHITE WINE

SERVES 2-4

INGREDIENTS:

2-3 pounds of mussels *(or clams, shrimp, or scallops)*

2 tablespoons extra virgin olive oil

5 garlic cloves, sliced

5 shallots, diced

1 teaspoon salt

1/2 teaspoon ground black pepper

4 plum tomatoes, diced *(or 1 can (15-16 ounces) diced tomatoes)*

1/2 cup white wine

1 stick of unsalted butter, cubed

Juice of 1 large lemon

1/4 cup grated Romano cheese

1/4 cup chopped fresh parsley

INSTRUCTIONS:

PREPARING THE MUSSELS:

Begin by washing the mussels in cold water. Pull off beards that hang from the shells. If any shells are open or cracked, discard the mussel.

COOKING THE MUSSELS:

In a large pot or skillet, add the extra virgin olive oil and bring to a high heat. Next, add in the garlic, shallots, salt, and ground black pepper and sauté for 3 minutes, mixing occasionally. Next, add in the mussels and cook until the shells begin to open slightly, about 4-5 minutes. Next, add in the tomatoes, white wine, unsalted butter, and lemon juice. Bring to a simmer and cook for 5 minutes, or until the tomatoes are soft. Finally, remove the skillet from the heat and add in the grated cheese and parsley.

TO SERVE:

Place mussels with the sauce in a large bowl or serving platter. Serve with toasted Italian bread.

APPROXIMATE PREP TIME: 10-15 minutes
APPROXIMATE COOK TIME: 10-15 minutes

SHRIMP SCAMPI

SERVES 4

INGREDIENTS:

2 pounds extra-large shrimp, rinsed with tails removed *(or 16 ounces scallops or 16 ounces calamari)*

1/4 cup extra virgin olive oil

4 garlic cloves, minced

1/2 teaspoon salt

1/2 teaspoon ground black pepper

1 stick of unsalted butter

1 cup white wine *(or seafood stock or vegetable broth)*

Juice of 1 lemon

1/4 cup fresh parsley

INSTRUCTIONS:

PREPARING THE SHRIMP:

In a large skillet, add the extra virgin olive oil and bring to a high heat. Next, add the garlic and sauté until golden, about 1-2 minutes. Next, add the shrimp, salt, and ground black pepper and sauté for 4 minutes, turning the shrimp over halfway through. Next, add the unsalted butter, white wine, lemon, and fresh parsley. Finally, bring to a simmer and cook for 4 minutes, mixing occasionally.

TO SERVE:

Place shrimp on a bed of your favorite cooked pasta (recommend spaghetti or linguini). Pour a spoonful of the desired amount of sauce over the shrimp.

APPROXIMATE PREP TIME: 10-15 minutes

APPROXIMATE COOK TIME: 10-15 minutes

Shrimp and Eggplant

SHRIMP AND EGGPLANT

SERVES 4

INGREDIENTS:

1 large or 2 medium eggplants *(or 2 zucchini or 1 bunch asparagus)*

1/4 cup extra virgin olive oil

1/2 teaspoon ground black pepper, divided

2 teaspoons salt, divided

1 pound uncooked spaghetti *(or your favorite pasta)*

1 stick unsalted butter

6 garlic cloves, sliced

1/2 cup vegetable broth

12-16 ounces large shrimp, rinsed with tails removed *(or 12 ounces scallops or 12 ounces squid)*

8 ounces fresh mozzarella, cut into 1/2-inch cubes

INSTRUCTIONS:

Pre-heat the oven to 400 degrees.

PREPARING THE EGGPLANT:

Begin by rinsing the eggplant and removing the ends. Next, cut the eggplant into 1-inch cubes and place in a mixing bowl or plastic bag. Next, add in the extra virgin olive oil, 1 teaspoon salt, and 1/4 teaspoon ground black pepper and mix well. Place the eggplant in a baking pan and roast at 400 degrees for 25 minutes. Remove the eggplant from the oven and set aside.

PREPARING THE PASTA:

While the eggplant is roasting, prepare the spaghetti according to the package instructions for al dente pasta. Strain the pasta and set aside.

SHRIMP AND EGGPLANT...CONTINUED

BRINGING EVERYTHING TOGETHER:

In a large pot or skillet, add in the unsalted butter and melt on medium heat. Next, add in the garlic and sauté until golden, about 1-2 minutes. Next, add in the shrimp, and the remaining 1 teaspoon of salt and 1/4 teaspoon of ground black pepper, and sauté for 2 minutes, mixing occasionally. Continuing on medium heat, add in the roasted eggplant and sauté for 2 minutes, mixing occasionally. Next, add in the spaghetti and vegetable broth and cook for 2 minutes, mixing occasionally, or until the spaghetti reaches the desired temperature. Finally, turn off the heat, add in the fresh mozzarella, and mix before serving.

TO SERVE:

Mix well to incorporate the fresh mozzarella. Serve once the mozzarella begins to melt.

APPROXIMATE PREP TIME: 20-30 minutes

APPROXIMATE COOK TIME: 50-60 minutes

INGREDIENT ALTERNATIVES

INGREDIENT	ALTERNATIVES
Artichoke Hearts	Hearts of Palm, Olives, Roasted Red Peppers, Tomatoes
Baccala (Cod)	Shrimp, Scallops, or Fillet of Fish
Beef Broth	Chicken Broth, Vegetable Broth, or Starchy Water
Bell Peppers	Roasted Red Peppers or Sun-Dried Tomatoes
Breadcrumbs	Flour, Corn Flakes (crushed), or Corn Meal
Broccoli	Peas, Spinach, Cauliflower, Eggplant, Zucchini, Broccoli Rabe or Asparagus
Broccoli Rabe	Spinach, Swiss Chard, Kale, or Broccoli
Butter	Extra Virgin Olive Oil
Calamari	Shrimp or Scallops
Cannellini beans	Great Northern, Navy, Kidney, or Pinto Beans
Canola Oil	Peanut or Avocado Oil
Cauliflower	Broccoli, Green Beans, Zucchini or Eggplant
Cavatelli	Ziti, Penne, Rigatoni, or Gemelli Pasta
Chicken Breasts	Pork Loin, Turkey Breast, or Fillet of Fish
Chicken Broth	Vegetable Broth, Beef Broth, or Starchy Water
Crushed Tomatoes	Tomato Puree or Whole Plum Tomatoes (crushed by hand)
Ditalini	Shells or Elbow Pasta

INGREDIENT	ALTERNATIVES
Eggplant	Zucchini, Yellow Squash, Broccoli, Asparagus, or Broccoli Rabe
Extra Virgin Olive Oil	Canola or Avocado Oil, or Butter
Farfalle	Ziti, Penne, Rigatoni, or Gemelli Pasta
Fontina Cheese	Swiss, Asiago, Provolone, or Mozzarella Cheese
Gemelli	Ziti, Penne, Farfalle, or Rigatoni Pasta
Gnocchi	Ravioli, Tortellini, or Cavatelli Pasta
Grape Tomatoes	Cherry Tomatoes (cut), Sun-Dried Tomatoes, Red Roasted Peppers
Green Beans	Zucchini, Spinach, Cauliflower, Broccoli, Asparagus, or Eggplant
Ground Beef	Ground Chicken, Pork, or Turkey
Heavy Cream	Light Cream or Half and Half
Kalamata Olives	Black or Green Olives
London Broil	Chicken Breasts, Turkey Breasts, or Boneless Pork Chops
Marinara Sauce	Vodka, Alfredo, or Roasted Tomato Sauce
Mozzarella Cheese (shredded)	Cheddar or Asiago
Mushrooms	Zucchini, Peas, Green Beans, Bell Pepper, or Beans
Mussels	Clams, Shrimp, or Scallops
Pancetta	Prosciutto, Bacon, or Ham

INGREDIENT	ALTERNATIVES
Parmesan Cheese (grated)	Asiago Cheese or Sharp Provolone
Penne	Ziti, Rigatoni, Farfalle, or Gemelli Pasta
Plum Tomatoes	Roasted Red Peppers, Sun-Dried Tomatoes, or Artichoke Hearts
Ravioli	Tortellini, Stuffed Shells, Gnocchi, or Manicotti Pasta
Red Onion	Sweet Onion, Shallots, Scallions, Leeks, or Green Onions
Red Potatoes	Yellow Potatoes, Purple Potatoes, or Fingerling Potatoes
Red Wine	White Wine, Balsamic Vinegar, Water, or Broth
Red Wine Vinegar	Balsamic, Apple Cider, or White Vinegar, or Pickle Juice
Ricotta Cheese	Cottage Cheese
Rigatoni	Ziti, Penne, Farfalle, or Gemelli Pasta
Roasted Red Peppers	Sun-Dried Tomatoes, Diced Tomatoes (can), Plum Tomatoes
Romano Cheese (grated)	Grated Parmesan or Asiago
Shrimp	Scallops or Calamari
Spaghetti	Linguine, Fettuccine, or Angel Hair Pasta
Sugar	Carrots minced
Sweet Dried Sausage	Sweet Dried Soppresatta or Pepperoni
Sweet Italian Sausage	Hot Italian, Chicken, or Turkey Sausage

INGREDIENT	ALTERNATIVES
Sweet Onion	Red Onion, Shallots, Scallions, Leeks, or Green Onions
Tortellini	Ravioli, Gnocchi, Cavatelli, Penne, Rigatoni, or Gemelli Pasta
Veal Cutlets	Chicken Breasts, Turkey Breasts, or Boneless Pork Chops
Vegetable Broth	Chicken Broth, Beef Broth, or Starchy Water
Vodka Sauce	Marinara, Alfredo, or Roasted Tomato Sauce
White Rice	Brown Rice, Quinoa, Bulgur Wheat, or Couscous
White Wine	Red Wine, Apple Cider Vinegar, Water, or Broth
Whole Milk	Light Cream or Half and Half
Yellow Squash	Zucchini, Eggplant, Green Beans, Broccoli, or Asparagus
Zucchini	Green Beans, Swiss Chard, Eggplant, or Asparagus

See more information about the author at
https://thomasjpapia.inventyourrecipe.com or scan the QR code below.

INDEX

Note: Italicized page numbers indicate photographs

A

Alfredo sauce, 9
Anchovy Pasta, 143
Appetizers. *See* Starters and Sides
Arancini, 16–17
Arancini Siciliano, *18*, 19–20
Artichokes, Stuffed, *47*, 48–49

B

Baked Ziti, 59, 60–61
Beans
    Chicken with Zucchini and Beans, 120
    Escarole and Beans, *25*, 26
    Pasta e Fagioli, *74*, 75
    Pork with Beans and Tomatoes, *132*, 133
    Tomato Soup, 53
Beef
    Beef and Broccoli, 125–126
    Beef Stew Italian Style, 124, *127*, 128
    Meatballs, 129–130
    Meatloaf Italian Style, 131
    Steak Pizzaiola, 136
Bolognese sauce, 10
Broccoli
    Beef and Broccoli, 125–126
    Cavatelli and Broccoli, 63
    Chicken Vodka with Broccoli, 118–119
    Creamy Pasta and Broccoli, 59, *64*, 65
    Farfalle with Sausage and Broccoli, *66*, 67–68
Broccoli Rabe
    about, 15
    as appetizer or side dish, 21
    Rigatoni and Broccoli Rabe, 79
    Sausage and Broccoli Rabe, 124, 134
Bruschetta, 22

C

Cacio e Pepe, 62
Cacuzza Stew, 15, *23*, 24
Calamari
    Calamari Marinara, 144
    Fried Calamari, 142, *146*, 147
Cauliflower, Fried, 27–28
Cavatelli and Broccoli, 63
Chicken
    about, 99
    Chicken Cacciatore, *100*, 101–102
    Chicken Francese, 103–104
    Chicken Margherita, 99, 105–106
    Chicken Marsala, 107–108
    Chicken Parmigiana, 109–110
    Chicken Piccata, 111–112
    Chicken Saltimbocca, 99, *115*, 116–117
    Chicken Vodka with Broccoli, 118–119
    Chicken with Roasted Red Peppers, 113–114
    Chicken with Zucchini and Beans, 120
    Stuffed Chicken Breasts, 121–122
Cod. See Fried Baccalà
Creamy Pasta and Broccoli, 59, *64*, 65

E

Eggplant
    about, 85
    Eggplant Casserole, 86–87

Eggplant Gemelli, 88–89
Eggplant Parmesan, 90–91, 92
Eggplant Rollatini, 85, *92*, 93–94
Eggplant Stacks, 85, *95*, 96–97
Shrimp and Eggplant, *150*, 151–152
Escarole and Beans, *25*, 26

F

Farfalle with Sausage and Broccoli, *66*, 67–68
Fish. *See* Seafood
Fried Baccalà, 142, 145
Fried Calamari, 142, *146*, 147
Fried Cauliflower, 27–28
Fried Ravioli, *29*, 30
Frittata, 31–32

G

Gnocchi Marinara, 69
Green Beans with Tomatoes and Garlic, 33
Ground Beef
    Arancini Siciliano, *18*, 19–20
    Baked Ziti, 59, 60–61
    Bolognese sauce, 10
    Lasagna with meat, 59, *70*, 71–72
    Meatballs, 129–130
    Meatloaf Italian Style, 131
    Spaghetti Bolognese, 80–81
    Stuffed Peppers, 51

I

Italian sausage. See Sausage

L

Lasagna with meat, 59, 70, 71–72

M

Macaroni Salad, 34
Marinara sauce, 11
Meat. *See* Beef; Pork; Veal
Meatballs, 129–130
Meatloaf Italian Style, 131
Mozzarella
    Mozzarella and Roasted Red Pepper Salad, 37
    Mozzarella and Tomato Salad, 38
    Mozzarella Caprese, *35*, 36
    Mozzarella Sticks, 39–40
Mushrooms, Stuffed, 50
Mussels and White Wine, 148

P

Pancetta
    Frittata, 31–32
    Pasta e Fagioli, *74*, 75
    Vodka sauce, 13
Pasta
    about, 59
    Anchovy Pasta, 143
    Baked Ziti, 59, 60–61
    Cacio e Pepe, 62
    Cavatelli and Broccoli, 63
    Creamy Pasta and Broccoli, 59, *64*, 65
    Eggplant Gemelli, 88–89
    Farfalle with Sausage and Broccoli, *66*, 67–68
    Gnocchi Marinara, 69
    Lasagna with meat, 59, *70*, 71–72
    Pasta Aglio e Olio, 59, 73
    Pasta e Fagioli, *74*, 75
    Pasta Primavera, 59, 76–77
    Penne a la Vodka, 78
    Rigatoni and Broccoli Rabe, 79
    Spaghetti Bolognese, 80–81

Spaghetti with Peppers and Onions, 82
Tortellini and Peas, 83
Penne a la Vodka, 78
Peppers
Chicken Cacciatore, *100*, 101–102
Chicken with Roasted Red Peppers, 113–114
Frittata, 31–32
Mozzarella and Roasted Red Pepper Salad, 37
Rotini Pasta Salad, 15, *44*, 45
Sausage with Peppers and Onions, 135
Spaghetti with Peppers and Onions, 82
Stuffed Peppers, 51
Veal and Peppers, 140
Peppers, Stuffed, 51
Pizza sauce, roasted tomato, 12
Pork
Farfalle with Sausage and Broccoli, *66*, 67–68
Pork with Beans and Tomatoes, *132*, 133
Sausage and Broccoli Rabe, 124, 134
Sausage with Peppers and Onions, 135
Potato Croquettes, 41–42
Potato Salad, 43
Poultry. *See* Chicken
Prosciutto
Chicken Saltimbocca, 99, *115*, 116–117
Veal with Prosciutto, 138–139

R
Ravioli, Fried, *29*, 30
Red Meat. *See* Beef; Pork; Veal
Rice balls
with cheese, 16–17
with meat, *18*, 19–20
Rigatoni and Broccoli Rabe, 79
Roasted tomato pizza sauce, 12
Rotini Pasta Salad, 15, *44*, 45

S
Salads
Macaroni Salad, 34
Mozzarella and Roasted Red Pepper Salad, 37
Mozzarella and Tomato Salad, 38
Potato Salad, 43
Rotini Pasta Salad, 15, *44*, 45
Tomato and Cucumber, 52
Tortellini Salad, *54*, 55
Sauces
about, 8
Alfredo, 9
Bolognese, 10
Marinara, 11
Roasted tomato pizza, 12
Vodka, 13
Sausage
Farfalle with Sausage and Broccoli, *66*, 67–68
Sausage and Broccoli Rabe, 124, 134
Sausage with Peppers and Onions, 135
Seafood
about, 142
Anchovy Pasta, 143
Calamari Marinara, 144
Fried Baccalà, 142, 145
Fried Calamari, 142, 147
Mussels and White Wine, 148
Shrimp and Eggplant, *150*, 151–152
Shrimp Scampi, 142, 149
Shellfish. See Seafood
Shrimp and Eggplant, *150*, 151–152
Shrimp Scampi, 142, 149
Soups
Tomato, 53
Spaghetti Bolognese, 80–81
Spaghetti with Peppers and Onions, 82

Spinach
- Chicken Saltimbocca, 99, *115*, 116–117
- Spinach with Tomatoes and Eggs, 46
- Stuffed Chicken Breasts, 121–122

Squid. *See* Calamari

Starters and Sides
- about, 15
- Arancini, 16–20
- Broccoli Rabe, 15, 21
- Bruschetta, 22
- Cacuzza Stew, 15, 24
- Escarole and Beans, 26
- Fried Cauliflower, 27–28
- Fried Ravioli, 30
- Frittata, 31–32
- Green Beans with Tomatoes and Garlic, 33
- Macaroni Salad, 34
- Mozzarella and Roasted Red Pepper Salad, 37
- Mozzarella and Tomato Salad, 38
- Mozzarella Caprese, 36
- Mozzarella Sticks, 39–40
- Potato Croquettes, 41–42
- Potato Salad, 43
- rice balls with cheese, 16–17
- rice balls with meat, 18–20
- Rotini Pasta Salad, 15, *44*, 45
- Spinach with Tomatoes and Eggs, 46
- Stuffed Artichokes, *47*, 48–49
- Stuffed Mushrooms, 50
- Stuffed Peppers, 51
- Tomato and Cucumber Salad, 52
- Tortellini Salad, 55
- Zucchini and Tomatoes, *56*, 57

Steak Pizzaiola, 136

Stews
- Beef Stew Italian Style, 124, 128

Stuffed Artichokes, *47*, 48–49
Stuffed Chicken Breasts, 121–122
Stuffed Mushrooms, 50
Stuffed Peppers, 51

T

Tomato(es)
- Bruschetta, 22
- Cacuzza Stew, 15, 24
- Green Beans with Tomatoes and Garlic, 33
- Mozzarella and Tomato Salad, 38
- Mozzarella Caprese, 36
- Pork with Beans and Tomatoes, *132*, 133
- Spinach with Tomatoes and Eggs, 46
- Tomato and Cucumber Salad, 52
- Tomato Soup, 53
- Zucchini and, *56*, 57

Tortellini and Peas, 83
Tortellini Salad, *54*, 55

V

Veal
- Veal and Peppers, 140
- Veal Cutlets, 137
- Veal with Prosciutto, 138–139

Vodka sauce, 13

Z

Zucchini
- Chicken with Zucchini and Beans, 120
- Zucchini and Tomatoes, *56*, 57

Printed in the USA
CPSIA information can be obtained
at www.ICGtesting.com
LVHW061946230424
778223LV00002B/2